"The more you get to know God, the more He will amaze you! In *The Jesus Mission*, Steven K. Scott shares the simple path that will get you on the right track."

> —MARK BATTERSON, lead pastor of National Community
> Church, Washington DC, and author of *Primal*
> and *In a Pit with a Lion on a Snowy Day*

"If you want to leave a positive legacy, *The Jesus Mission* gives you the road map you need. I highly recommend it."

> —GARY CHAPMAN, PhD, best-selling author of *The Five*
> *Love Languages* and *Love as a Way of Life*

"*The Jesus Mission* gets straight to the point of Christ's mission to set the captives free. It will change your life and empower you to make an impact in the lives of others that will last for eternity."

> —NICK VUJICIC, evangelist and author of *Life Without Limits*

"Be prepared for something incredible to happen as you experience Christ's words penetrating your heart. Steven K. Scott does a masterful job of helping us grasp the close relationship with God that we deeply desire."

> —DR. CHUCK LYNCH, author of *I Should Forgive, But…*

"In *The Jesus Mission*, you will see the Savior as you have never seen Him before. Any misconceptions about who He was, why He came, and what He wants His followers to do and to be will be replaced with His truth, according to the words He spoke. It's time to make His priorities our priorities!"

> —DR. TIMOTHY CLINTON, president of the American
> Association of Christian Counselors

"Steven K. Scott provides a practical and doable path to living each day supernaturally. His chapter describing how to experience intimacy with God is profound, yet so clear. It all is based on Jesus' words. If you have ever wanted a comprehensive handbook on what it means to be a follower of Jesus Christ, you are holding it in your hands."

—Dr. David Stoop, author of *You Are What You Think* and founder of the Center for Family Therapy

THE
JESUS
MISSION

Christ completed 27 missions while on earth.
Take up the 4 He assigned to you.

THE
JESUS
MISSION

STEVEN K.
SCOTT

WATERBROOK
PRESS

THE JESUS MISSION
PUBLISHED BY WATERBROOK PRESS
12265 Oracle Boulevard, Suite 200
Colorado Springs, Colorado 80921

ISBN 978-0-307-73049-7
ISBN 978-0-307-73050-3 (electronic)

Cover design by Mark D. Ford

Published in the United States by WaterBrook Multnomah, an imprint of the Crown Publishing Group, a division of Random House Inc., New York.

WATERBROOK and its deer colophon are registered trademarks of Random House Inc.

Library of Congress Cataloging-in-Publication Data
Scott, Steve, 1948-
    The Jesus mission : Christ completed twenty-seven missions while on earth : take up the four he assigned to you / Steven K. Scott.
        p. cm.
    Includes bibliographical references (p.   ).
    ISBN 978-0-307-73049-7 — ISBN 978-0-307-73050-3 (electronic)
    1. Christian life. I. Title.
    BV4501.3.S3935 2011
    248.4—dc23
                            2011021538

Printed in the United States of America
2011—First Edition

10 9 8 7 6 5 4 3 2 1

To the King of kings and Lord of lords,
the One who paid the ultimate price that no one else could pay and
freely gave me that which cost Him everything. Oh what a Savior!
To my Heavenly Father,
who willingly gave the One He loved above all others
for those of us who didn't even care.
How can You love us so? Let me love You and Your dear Son
the way You desire to be loved.
To the Holy Spirit,
whose ministry has delivered the miracle of the second birth
to millions since that glorious day He was sent to earth.

To my sweet wife, Shannon,
who selflessly supports every aspect of my life and ministry,
has a selfless love for our family,
and is my wonderful example of someone with a true,
childlike faith in the Lord.
To my children and grandchildren:
May following Christ and living in true intimacy with God be
your diligent pursuit and experience throughout your lives on earth.
To Jim Shaughnessy and Gary Smalley:
Oh how God has used you both
to make me want to be more like Jesus!
To Pastor Keith Craft:
Your life, ministry, faith, and prayers have made
an eternal difference in every aspect of my life and ministry.

And this is eternal life, that they may
know You, the only true God,
and Jesus Christ whom You have sent.

—Jesus

CONTENTS

PART 3:
WHAT YOU NEVER KNEW ABOUT JESUS THAT WILL CHANGE YOUR LIFE

ACKNOWLEDGMENTS

My wonderful partners at Random House Inc. and WaterBrook Multnomah. Steve Cobb, thank you for your efforts to make this project a reality. Ron Lee, as always, your editing and wisdom have made such an invaluable contribution to the readability and ultimate impact of this book. To the marketing, sales, ministry, and design teams at WaterBrook. Without your efforts this book would never be read. I am so grateful for you all!

Jan Miller, you are such a gift to me and to all whom you represent. Your wisdom, professionalism, faith, and energy are the reasons our works are published and taken seriously. For me, you are truly irreplaceable!

THE

JESUS
MISSION

CHAPTER 1

THE GREATEST MISSION THE UNIVERSE HAS EVER WITNESSED

If Jesus were to fail, the earth and everyone on it would be doomed.

About two thousand years ago, all the hosts of heaven watched in amazement as God sent His only begotten Son on a mission. While living on earth, God's Son would take on the form of a man and give up His divine rights. As a man, He would be tempted in every area of life in which ordinary men and women are tempted. If the Son succumbed to even one temptation, His mission would be aborted, and the earth and its inhabitants would be doomed.

Though He lived as a man, the Son's communion with His Father remained unbroken. His obedience to the Father's will was nothing short of perfect. The close communion He enjoyed with His Father was crucial to the successful completion of His mission.

But the Son's mission on earth was *not* just one mission. In His teachings, He revealed that He came to accomplish twenty-seven seemingly impossible missions. If He failed in even one, all would be lost. Each of the twenty-seven missions had to be completed, and without error, during His brief life on earth. And amazingly, He did it!

THE MISSIONS JESUS GAVE TO US

While most Christians are familiar with the Great Commission from Matthew 28:19–20, which is Jesus' command to make disciples of all nations, many may be unaware that before Jesus left the earth, He commissioned His disciples—and everyone else who would follow Him in the future—not with just one Great Commission, but with four lifelong missions that all believers are to focus on.

As believers, we often struggle with what God wants from our lives. What is His specific will for each of us, and how should we invest our lives to advance His work on earth? Jesus did not leave us in the dark, to guess at what God desires for us. The missions He left for us to carry out give us eternal purpose and a clear focus for our lives. As we pursue the four missions He gave us, we will experience the ultimate Christian life.

Far from being overwhelming, these missions sharpen our focus and intensify our faith. Out of all the opportunities and possibilities that believers could pursue, Christ points us to the missions He chose for us. There is no reason for believers to guess about what God wants or to worry that they are not hearing from God. In His teachings, Jesus has already revealed it all.

In the words of Christ from the four gospels, we have our job description. Jesus chose to give *us* the glorious opportunity to *partner* with Him in the same way that He partnered with His Father. As we pursue the four lifelong missions, He gives us His miraculous power and grace to fulfill each one. Jesus said, "Anyone who has faith in me will do what I have been doing. He will do even greater things than these, because I am going to the Father" (John 14:12).

As we carry out our missions, we will live in an intimate relationship with Him that is modeled after His relationship with His Father. Just as Jesus relied on His Father and drew wisdom and power from Him, so can believers today draw near to Christ in the most intimate relationship on earth. This is not restricted to a few special Christians or limited to the most holy. Jesus invites all His followers into an intimate relationship that mirrors the relationship He experienced with His Father when He was on earth.

Before we look at this relationship with Christ, there are a few realities we need to consider.

BETTER THAN A CRYSTAL BALL

It's tempting to think that life would be much easier if only we could know what lies ahead. If we had a crystal ball that would allow us to see into the future, we could take the risk and uncertainty out of decision making. Think about it: you could win the lottery *every week*. If you're an investor, you could read tomorrow's *Wall Street Journal* today and make a fortune overnight. You could steer clear of traffic jams and dangerous motorists. You could ensure good health by avoiding the threats of disease and disaster. If only you had a crystal ball, you could become your company's most valued employee by next week—and without relying on hard work and business acumen.

No longer would you be uncertain or indecisive. With an infallible crystal ball, you could see the long-term benefits and consequences of every decision and choice. You would have the potential to avoid making mistakes in every area of your life.

But that is all it would be—potential. That's because you would still be lacking one critical element. Even if you knew everything you needed to know about the future, you still would not have the *power* to change your life. You would not have the will to do the right thing in every instance, and you would still be subject to circumstances over which you have no control.

Knowing the future would not replace sadness with joy, emptiness with fulfillment, or death with eternal life. It would not eliminate the guilt you experience when you do something wrong. It could not empower you to love others unconditionally. For all the changes a future-seeing crystal ball could bring, it couldn't bring the most important changes that you need or desire. And worst of all, it could not bring you even one step closer to an intimate relationship with an eternal, infinite God.

What you will discover in this book is infinitely better than a crystal ball. You won't be able to read the future, but you will find out how you can enjoy the most intimate, powerful, and miracle-filled relationship possible with God. This relationship, which Christ offers to us, *can* replace sadness with joy, emptiness with fulfillment, failure with accomplishment, and most important, death with eternal life. Imagine having a relationship with

God in which He reveals Himself to you in new ways every day. He will reveal His loves and desires, His values, and even His miraculous power in unique ways—to you, one of His closest followers.

Imagine experiencing Christ's presence every moment of every day. Imagine being so close to Him that He whispers in your ear His thoughts, His guidance, even His perfect will for every decision you face. Imagine knowing that you are the focal point of His amazing love. In turn, you will gain the power to love others unconditionally in ways you never thought were possible. Imagine gaining the power to love and forgive even the people who have lied about you, betrayed you, and violated your trust.

This is the life of power and supernatural love that Christ lived on earth, and it can be your life as well. When you live in an intimate relationship with Him, He teaches you how to abide in His love and power. He directs your steps and opens your eyes to choices and decisions that produce a life of eternal significance.

GETTING OUT OF THE WATER BEFORE IT'S TOO LATE

Imagine that you are alone in a small rowboat. You have only one oar and no sail. If you are floating on a quiet lake and not drifting a great distance from shore, you should be able to make your way back to dry land. That is, unless a storm erupts and pushes you in the opposite direction.

Most people assume their lives should go smoothly, with only minor interruptions and reasonable obstacles to overcome. They don't see why they should have to deal with major setbacks such as serious illness or financial misfortune. They expect a life of steady progress, with few detours and with the support of close relationships.

I see this all the time. Many go about their daily lives with little sense of direction and purpose, expecting success but not making the sacrifices necessary to achieve their goals. They don't realize that the dam that lies beyond their field of vision is about to break. The quiet mountain lake will suddenly turn into a raging torrent that will pull everything on the lake to the breach in the dam. The current will force the rowboat and its occupant over the broken dam. That destiny will be inescapable.

Your life can seem to be as peaceful and nonthreatening as a quiet lake. But a life that appears to be a comfortable refuge, protected from adversity, is never what it seems. No one is spared the hard realities of life on earth. The only real question facing us is, when will the dam break?

Most of us expect the status quo to remain. We have no sense of urgency pushing us to refocus our lives on what is most important. We justify the way we live by saying, "I'm doing okay. Surely God doesn't expect *that* much more from me." We find it easy to compare ourselves to others who make worse choices than we make. "Maybe I'm not Billy Graham, but I'm not Adolf Hitler either." Oddly, we feel good about landing somewhere in the middle. "If God grades on the curve, I'm probably between a C+ and a B-."

Here's the truth. God *doesn't* grade on a curve. He sees you as you really are. He knows your words and actions, your true motives, and the intentions behind everything you do and think. Even more, He measures your actions, words, and motives against *His* standards, which reflect His perfect righteousness. Jesus gave us a glimpse of God's perfect standards when He said if you have been angry with someone, you are just as guilty as one who committed murder (see Matthew 5:21–22). If you have failed to love your neighbor in the same manner and degree that you love yourself, then by the standard of God's love, you have *not* loved your neighbor.

And here is something many have missed that prevents them from experiencing the ultimate intimate relationship with God. If we don't love God in the way *He* wants to be loved, then our love for Him is worthless. Ouch! That's bad news for all of us. But the great news is that He loves you and me anyway! He loves us so much that He has made the ultimate sacrifice (the death of His Son) to bring you and me into a miraculous, love-drenched, eternal relationship with Him.

The Four-Dollar Frame with a Hidden Treasure

As he walked through a Pennsylvania flea market in 1989, a young man picked up an old painting that was for sale. He later described it as "dreary," but he liked the ornate frame and thought he could find a print to replace the ugly painting. And the price was only four dollars.

When he got home and started to remove the frame's backing, the frame fell apart. He was upset at first but then noticed a folded piece of paper that had been tucked beneath the painting's backing. It appeared to be a printed copy of the Declaration of Independence. It was in such good condition, however, that he thought it must have been put there by a recent owner.

The buyer of the painting was wrong. This copy of the Declaration of Independence was produced by a printer named John

Dunlap at the request of Alexander Hamilton and the Continental Congress on the night of July 4, 1776. It was one of an estimated two hundred copies that were printed to be circulated in the thirteen colonies. By 1989, there were only twenty-four copies known to exist, and this was one of the three most pristine. This copy of the Declaration had been hidden right after it was printed, because to be caught with a copy would result in being hanged as a traitor. The man who purchased a frame and a dreary painting for $4 sold a rare copy of the Declaration of Independence for $2.4 million. A few years later it sold at auction for $8 million.

The previous owner of the ugly painting, who sold it for four dollars, had made the greatest financial mistake of his life. His error was that he had assumed the worth of the painting was limited to what could be seen. But as the flea market customer realized later, the true value was determined by what was hidden on the inside—that which could *not* be seen.

How do you value yourself? By your physical appearance, income, possessions, or job title? We all tend to measure our success, the quality of our lives, and our worth by the things that can be seen—the same mistake that was made by the previous owner of the ugly painting in the ornate frame. The truth is that we *all* resemble that old painting in the ornate frame. The painting is our nature that has been beaten up, bruised, and blurred by years of disappointment, hurts, and self-centeredness. The ornate frame represents the external features of our lives, which we rely on to try to appear more important and valuable. But hidden beneath it all are our souls, hopelessly trapped by self-centeredness and our sin nature.

We would be lost but for one thing. Standing nearby is God

Himself. His vision for you and me is not limited by outward appearance, lack of the trappings of success, or our inborn self-centeredness. God said, "For the LORD does not see as man sees; for man looks at the outward appearance, but the LORD looks at the heart" (1 Samuel 16:7, NKJV).

As you read the chapters that follow, you will discover how God wants to liberate your soul and give you an eternal Declaration of Independence. You will see that He desires to set you free to be all that He designed you to be. And just as the Declaration of Independence created a new nation with an unparalleled destiny, when God sets you free, your destiny will not only change, but it will also take on eternal significance in your life and the lives of countless others.

THE CORE OF CHRISTIAN FAITH

We can live in an intimate relationship with God only because of what Christ has done. None of this would be possible if He had not first accomplished all the missions He was given. Imagine, a God who loves you so much that He sent His Son on a mission to rescue and liberate *you*! This is the God you are going to come to know and love more intimately than you have ever imagined possible.

The Jesus Mission will take you to the core of Christian faith, clarifying what God wants from your life and showing you the difference between subscribing to a religious belief and actually following Jesus as He desires. This book is broken into three sections, with each one exploring what Jesus taught, promised, and commanded. *The Jesus Mission* builds from the starting point (being born again and experiencing real intimacy with God), to the four missions Christ has given us (what God wants from your life), to the way Jesus reveals Himself and the work He did on earth (the twenty-seven impossible missions He accomplished).

We'll start at the beginning. In part 1 you will learn from the words of Christ exactly how God wants to be loved and how *you* can live in an intimate love relationship with Him.

PART 1

INTIMACY WITH GOD, THE WAY *HE* WANTS IT

CHAPTER 2

THE FOUR MOST IMPORTANT QUESTIONS YOU WILL EVER ASK

You can't truly love God unless you love Him according to His desires.

I am a pragmatic, results-oriented businessman who discovers breakthrough products—products that do things nothing else can do. Then my companies acquire the worldwide marketing rights to the new products, and we build businesses around them. Our efforts have been blessed beyond measure, resulting in billions of dollars in sales. As a very practical entrepreneur, I have no time to spend on anything that is *not* what it purports to be. I'm not interested in theories or good ideas. I invest my efforts only in the things that are absolutely real.

The life of faith is no less important. No one wants to spend time pursuing superstition, mistaken beliefs, or ineffective practices. Doing so is not only a waste of time but a waste of one's life. In my pursuit of God, I want to do things His way.

Jesus is not a mythical figure from history who I *hope* is real. During the past forty-six years, I have experienced a relationship with Christ that is as real as my relationships with my wife, my children, and my best friends. I have experienced countless events that even the most skeptical onlookers would have to classify as miracles. My purpose here is *not* to persuade you that Christ is real. My purpose is to share who Jesus *really* is—what He is like, what He loves, and what He hates. I also will share why He came to earth two thousand years ago and, most important, what it means for you.

WHAT THIS WILL DO FOR YOU

When I speak to audiences about the realities of Jesus Christ and my relationship with Him, I often hear comments such as "I wish my relationship with the Lord was more real" or "I don't feel like I'm nearly as close to Him as I want to be." People wonder why God seems distant and why He is not more involved in their lives. People tell me, "I just wish I could *know* He's hearing my prayers" and "If only I could see Him face to face for just a couple of minutes."

Every year I speak to thousands of men and women at churches and Christian conferences. I nearly always ask, "How many of you wish you could have a more intimate relationship with God?" Nearly everyone will raise their hand!

How would you answer if I asked you that question? Do you wish you could have a more real and more intimate relationship with God? The great news is you *can*! There is nothing God wants more than for you to start living in an intimate relationship with Him. As you read this book, you will discover what to do to enjoy the intimacy with God that you have wanted for so long. And you won't learn it from me; you will learn it from the Lord Jesus Himself.

You will have the opportunity to experience a life-transforming relationship with Christ. It will be more powerful than falling in love, getting married, raising your children, or enjoying time with your best friend. You can enter into a tangible relationship with God that goes deeper than any other.

In human terms, the greatest love we experience is love for our children. And yet, the love for God that grows in your heart can surpass even the love of a parent. I recently met a forty-two-year-old believer from Romania named Beni Lup. After hearing his story, my heart bonded with him. And Beni, his family, and the Christians of Romania became my new heroes of faith.

CHRISTIANS WHO KNOW GOD INTIMATELY

Ion Vasile was a Romanian soldier during World War II. On a battlefield he heard Americans in a trench singing hymns. He and a number of other Romanian soldiers made their way to the American trenches to meet the men who were singing. Not only did the GIs share the gospel with the Romanians; they gave them their pocket hymnals.

Ion experienced firsthand the love of God as he heard of God's grace and mercy and the sacrifice made by God's Son for *Ion's* sin. He surrendered his life to Christ and committed the *rest* of his life to following Him. After the war he returned home to his wife, Ceta, and their eight children. They started an underground church in their village that grew to a congregation of twenty-five within one year. By then, Romania had been taken over by Communists. As the new regime gained control of the nation, Christian meetings were outlawed, and Christians were terrorized. Without warning, believers were seized from their homes, sometimes never to be seen again. And those who did return bore scars from the brutal torture they had endured.

Romanian Christians had no choice but to gather secretly to worship God in homes. With curtains drawn and light from a single candle, they silently mouthed the words of hymns and studied God's Word.

One of Ion's daughters, Lia, married a believer named Nelu Lup. After years of trying to conceive a child, they learned from a doctor that Lia would never be able to become pregnant. Upon receiving this heartbreaking news, Ion, Ceta, Lia, and Nelu prayed for a miracle. They promised the Lord that if He would intervene and give Lia and Nelu a child, that child would be dedicated to the Lord's service. Lia became pregnant, and on July 20, 1969, as the world watched Neil Armstrong take his first step on the moon, Lia gave birth to a son they named Beni.

Under the Communist regime, Bibles were outlawed. If you were caught with one, you could be thrown in prison. If you were caught distributing Bibles, you were sure to go to prison, where you would be tortured, and most likely you would never be seen again. And yet the Romanian Christians treasured nothing as much as a Bible.

When Beni was a child, Bibles were hidden near the Lup home. Beni's dad would retrieve the package of Bibles and place it in young Beni's backpack. In the morning, as the boy walked through the countryside to school, he would climb a hill and bury the Bibles under a tree. The Lups never knew who left Bibles for them to deliver, nor did they know who recovered the Bibles that Beni buried. Yet this went on for years.

Years later Beni's father told him, "Every time I watched you begin your walk up that hill, I felt what Abraham must have felt as he took Isaac up the mountain to be sacrificed. I *knew* that if anyone saw you, you would be taken, and I would never see you again. Every day I had to choose to love God more than my only son. And every day God reminded me that He had sacrificed His one and only Son for us. As you walked out of view, my heart was breaking. But every afternoon you came back home. Oh how I love God!"

This is the kind of relationship with God I am talking about. Not simply a religious philosophy to discuss or a ritual of religious formalities to follow. I'm talking about a relationship with God that is so real and so personal that when you experience it, it becomes more important than anything or anyone else in your life.

A CLEAR UNDERSTANDING OF JESUS CHRIST

In a later chapter we will discuss the most common misconceptions about Jesus. For example, many people believe that Jesus wanted to start a new religion. Others are convinced He was a Gandhi-like figure who was consumed by notions of social justice and changing the plight of the poor.

I am appalled when people take a handful of Jesus' statements out of context and twist them to support their own positions that are completely contrary to His teachings. It seems that every group wants to claim Jesus as the cheerleader for its pet cause. This is done by political groups, religious groups, charitable groups, and various causes and campaigns. But Jesus does not give us that option. He did not come to earth to join anyone's group or to carry the banner for anyone's cause, no matter how noble that cause may be. To the contrary, He came to call us to join *His* cause, to become *His* followers, and to serve in *His* kingdom. He said, "If anyone desires to come after Me, let him deny himself, and take up his cross, and follow Me" (Matthew 16:24, NKJV).

No one has to guess who Jesus is and what He stands for. He has told us in His nineteen hundred statements recorded in the New Testament. Unfortunately, most people—even those who say they believe in Jesus—are unaware of many of His teachings.

ACTING ON WHAT YOU KNOW

Just as important as what you believe about Jesus is what you *do* in response to who He is and what He said. In later chapters we will look at the twenty-seven specific missions that Jesus came to earth to accomplish and the four missions that He assigned to us. But we can't live the life that God promises us if we don't first understand Jesus as the Scriptures reveal Him. For example, people are led to believe that because God is a God of love, He really doesn't care if we do what He commands. God's love, grace, and mercy certainly exceed the limits of our imagination. But so do His righteousness and justice. The same Jesus who said, "For God so loved the world that He gave His only begotten Son, that whoever believes in Him should not perish but have everlasting life" (John 3:16, NKJV) also said, "Not everyone who says to Me, 'Lord, Lord,' shall enter the kingdom of heaven, but he who *does* the will of My Father in heaven" (Matthew 7:21, NKJV). He then warned those who were the most religious: "Many will say to Me in that day, 'Lord, Lord, have we not prophesied in Your name, cast out demons in Your name, and done many wonders in Your name?' And then I will declare to them, 'I never knew you; depart from Me, you who practice lawlessness!'" (Matthew 7:22–23, NKJV). Because so many people are not aware of everything Jesus said, they are lax about obeying His teachings. And they are quick to remake Him into a Santa Claus god of their own design.

But Jesus does not give us that option. To have an intimate relationship with Christ, our only choice is to follow Him on His terms. And He is the One who sets the terms.

If you haven't decided whether you want a relationship with God, you will have a chance to see Jesus as He really is. You will learn what He said is needed to receive God's gift of eternal life. You'll discover His secrets for having your prayers answered and how you can experience a greater level of joy and peace than anything you have experienced before. And with all the violence, unrest, deadly disasters, and war in the world, wouldn't it be wonderful to be free of worry and fear?

You may wonder why I feel qualified to state who Jesus really is and what He requires from us. I'll tell you. In addition to my forty-six-year relationship with Christ and countless hours of Bible study, I spent two years doing what no other person had done before—I organized *all* of Jesus' statements (more than nineteen hundred) into 225 topics and made them available in a book. *The Greatest Words Ever Spoken*[1] gives readers the opportunity to read Jesus' words on every subject He addressed and to get to know Him on His terms. As a result of going over each of His nineteen hundred statements again and again for two years, I became intimately aware of how His teachings fit together and gained the big picture of why He came to earth, what He preached and taught, and the whole of His teachings, topic by topic.

Why is a topical arrangement of His words so helpful in understanding His character, His missions, and His requirements? Let me give you an analogy.

The Ultimate Set of Jigsaw Puzzles

Imagine if I showed up at your house with boxes containing 225 jigsaw puzzles. When assembled, each puzzle will create a wonderful picture. Now imagine that rather than assembling the puzzles one at a time, we dumped all the pieces of all 225 puzzles onto the floor. You would have hundreds of separate pieces, and each piece would have color, shape, and a purpose. But as long as the puzzle pieces are left in a pile, you would only be able to *guess* what picture the puzzle maker wanted to convey. And virtually anyone could pick up any puzzle piece and say anything they wanted to say about that piece.

For example, you could pick up a blue piece and say it was part of a lake. But when you fit it into the puzzle, it turns out to be blue sky reflected in the windows of an office tower. You think it's simply a puzzle of a beautiful sunny day. But the beauty of the scene is shattered when you add another puzzle piece. Now you realize this is a picture of terror. Approaching the sky-blue wall of this office tower is a Boeing 767. This puzzle does not form a picture of a beautiful sunny day in New York City; it is a picture of the World Trade Center on September 11, 2001.

You see, to understand the artist's message, you have to see the *whole* picture. And to do that, every piece must be considered and given its place in the picture as a whole.

As I organized the statements of Jesus into 225 topics, I saw for the first time the whole picture of what He was saying, subject by subject. When you step back and take it in, seeing His entire teaching on a subject is incredibly powerful. If someone takes a verse from the Bible out of context, it can be misinterpreted and misrepresented. But the clear picture that is formed by Christ's teachings taken all together (and on each topic) can *not* be misinterpreted or manipulated. A person's opinion and bias cannot overcome the clear meaning of Jesus' words—addressing the subjects He considered most important—when they are looked at together.

FROM ATHEISM TO FOLLOWING CHRIST

By the age of fifteen, I had become what the reformers called a "practical atheist." I thought there was a possibility that the Bible could be true, but only a slight possibility. More convincing to me were the questions I had about the existence of God that no one had been able to answer. As far as I was concerned, God was as mythical as Santa Claus.

One night shortly before I turned sixteen, I met George Byer, a former atheist who had become a believer in God and a dedicated follower of Jesus Christ. That night he confronted me with the reality of Jesus Christ.

George was the head chemical engineer for one of the largest aerospace firms in America. He didn't talk to me about religion; he didn't even present a religious argument in favor of belief. Instead, he explained that God didn't want a *religion* to come between me and Him. Rather, God wanted an intimate and dynamic personal relationship with me. As wonderful as this sounded, there was one giant roadblock. I couldn't believe that an eternal, infinite God existed.

George asked if I would read a book he wanted to give me. I asked, "How thick is the book?" He said it was about a half-inch thick. That sounded pretty easy, so I agreed, and he ran to his car and brought back a copy of *Mere Christianity*. This is the classic argument for God's existence by atheist-turned-Christian C. S. Lewis. Less than a week later, I found myself believing that Jesus *was* the Person He claimed to be—the only begotten Son of the living God.

That was in 1964, and in the forty-seven years that have followed, Jesus has proved Himself in a thousand ways, including the incredible miracles that He has performed in my life. In spite of all my failings, He has always been there. I know that He's real, not because of my hope or belief, but because of the tangible experiences I've had with Him. He never fails to demonstrate His love, mercy, and grace in and around my life. In a later chapter I will share a number of events that can't be explained by anything other than the work of an infinite God. One dramatic example was the instant disappearance of my son's cancer, which the surgeons and their team could only call "a miracle."

My goal in writing this book is simple: to help you answer the four most important questions you can ask, and to offer you a simple path that can result in a level of intimacy with God that is more real, more life changing, and more miraculous than you have imagined possible. This is a path that was authored by God the Father and announced, demonstrated, and illuminated by Jesus Christ.

THE FOUR QUESTIONS THAT WILL DEFINE YOUR RELATIONSHIP WITH GOD

Everyone who seriously considers the question of God's existence, and all who want to know Christ in an intimate relationship, must find the answers to four questions:

1. What does God want from you?
2. How can you give God what He wants?
3. Who is Jesus?
4. Why did Jesus come to earth?

The answers to the first two questions open a path to experiencing a deeper level of intimacy with God and the miracles that accompany such an intimate relationship with Him. The answers to the last two questions will surprise and shock a lot of people and will expose common misconceptions about Jesus and His missions on earth. He did not come here to establish a new religion, and He was not a social reformer or a champion of earthly equality. Jesus revealed the twenty-seven missions that He came to accomplish, which we will look at later. We also will look more closely at the evidence of His divinity and the saving work Christ did on the cross.

You do not have to take a leap of blind faith to believe in Jesus. There is more than enough evidence to convince even the most hardened skeptic. The beliefs of your heart begin in your mind. Many people have not gained a saving faith in Christ because their minds have never been fully exposed to the truths about Him and the truths He revealed when He was on earth.

If you are on the fence, or if you are holding back in ways that prevent you from knowing Christ in an intimate relationship, consider this: *If* Jesus is who He claimed to be, His words would be absolute truth. Therefore, discovering what He said about you, your life, and your eternal destiny is more important than any other information you will ever consider! Christ's words answer the core questions of your life: Why am I here? What is my purpose on earth? Is it possible to gain eternal life, and if so, how?

These are just a few of the questions Jesus answered about you and me. And if He is God (as He claimed), then His answers are the final word.

In later chapters we will examine compelling proofs of His deity. There is so much proof, in fact, that when the evidence is considered, a person must choose to be intellectually dishonest to continue to reject Him.

One of the most important truths that Jesus revealed was that the God of the universe wants to have an intimate relationship with you. So get ready for the most wonderful ride of your life! A ride full of awe and wonder, of power and direction, that can change your life and the lives of those you love, forever.

CHAPTER 3

WHAT DOES GOD
WANT FROM YOU?

*There is no more important
question you can ask.*

According to a 2007 Gallup poll, about 86 percent of all Americans say they believe in God, and 81 percent say they believe in the existence of heaven.[2] I would assume that, since you are reading this book, you count yourself among those who believe in the existence of God. That's good news, because people can't discover what God wants from them if they doubt He exists. The writer of Hebrews said it this way: "But without faith it is *impossible* to please Him, for he who comes to God must believe that He is, and that He is a rewarder of those who diligently seek Him" (11:6, NKJV).

Unfortunately, our modern use of the words *believe* and *faith* is radically different from their meaning in the Bible. When we say we believe something, we mean that we acknowledge it to be true. We are assenting intellectually to a premise or statement. But when Jesus or the apostles used the word *believe,* they meant something very different. They equated belief or faith with an attitude of *total commitment* that was acknowledged in one's thinking and *also* was embraced completely by the heart. Belief in the first century went to the core of a person's being. Jesus said that *all* our behavior, whether good or bad, flows out of our hearts. So our behavior always reflects what is at our core, the true beliefs of our hearts.

The root Greek word that Jesus and the apostles used that is translated into the English words *believe, belief,* and *faith* is *pisteuo,* which means to "totally rely upon." So while most Americans acknowledge that they "believe" in God on some level, by God's definition of *belief* and *faith,* the only people who *really* believe are those who totally rely on Him. Said another way, by God's definition, the only people who truly believe in Him are those who make their relationship with Him their number-one priority. Their actions demonstrate their belief by making God's Word the primary determining factor of their behavior. Measured by God's standard, most of those who say they believe in Him have a shallow belief at best.

BAD NEWS, GOOD NEWS

No matter what we *say* we believe, our hearts and our actions express what we *really* believe. Addressing this, Jesus said, "You are the ones who justify yourselves in the eyes of men, but God knows your hearts. What is highly valued among men is detestable in God's sight" (Luke 16:15). And toward the end of His Sermon on the Mount, Jesus made a shocking revelation—one that should concern many who consider themselves believers in God and followers of Christ. He said, "Therefore by their fruits [behavior] you will know them. Not everyone who says to Me, 'Lord, Lord,' shall enter the kingdom of heaven, but he who *does* the will of My Father in heaven. Many will say to Me in that day, 'Lord, Lord, have we not prophesied in Your name, cast out demons in Your name, and done many wonders in Your name?' And then I will declare to them, 'I never knew you; depart from Me, you who practice lawlessness!'" (Matthew 7:20–23, NKJV).

The bad news is that it doesn't matter how *we* define belief and saving faith. We are not the final authorities in matters of faith and salvation. God looks at our hearts, so the issue is, what do we truly believe in our hearts, at the core of our being? Do our choices and behavior reflect hearts that love God and love what He loves? Are His values and priorities *our* values and priorities? Are we bearing spiritual fruit that is consistent with hearts that believe in Him? These are critical questions that every one of us needs to ask—because according to Jesus, our eternal destiny will be determined by the beliefs of our hearts, not mere mental agreement with theological statements or doctrines.

Now here's the good news! Regardless of where your heart is right now, it can be transformed into the heart God wants it to be, instantly! And the best news is that He, not you, is the One who will miraculously transform your heart. (That is the focus of the next chapter.) But for now, let's discover exactly *what* He wants from you and me.

The Great News

The greatest news you can hear is that God doesn't make us guess what He wants. In both the Old and New Testaments, He makes it perfectly clear. For instance, He tells us in Jeremiah 9:23–24:

> Thus says the LORD: "Let not the wise man glory in
>   his wisdom,
> Let not the mighty man glory in his might,
> Nor let the rich man glory in his riches;
> *But let him who glories glory in this,*
> *That he understands and knows Me,*
> That I am the LORD, exercising lovingkindness, judgment,
>   and righteousness in the earth.
> For in these I delight," says the LORD. (NKJV)

Imagine—the infinite God, the Creator of the universe, wants *you* to understand who He really is and what He loves. But He doesn't stop there. He wants you to have an *intimate* relationship with Him. In the passage from Jeremiah, the Hebrew word that is translated "knows" is a word that literally means "to *intimately* know." In other places in the Old Testament, the same word is used to describe the intimacy a man and a woman experience when they consummate their marriage. God wants to be that intimate, and *more,* in His relationship with you and me!

Here's the best news of all. As much as you may want this kind of relationship with God, *He* wants it even more—infinitely more! In fact, He wants it so much that He sent His only begotten Son to earth to live a sinless life and then to be sacrificed on the cross to pay the debt of your sin. In dying for you, Christ created the only way you can have intimacy with God the Father and with His Son. Though He offers this relationship at no cost to us, it cost Him everything!

Added to the deepest intimacy possible in any relationship, God tells us that He wants our intimacy with Him to be the "glory" of our lives. This relationship is to be our joy and our overriding purpose.

When my son Ryan was sixteen, he qualified to compete in the National Junior Olympics Track and Field Championships in the high jump. Out of forty-five jumpers who qualified, Ryan went in ranked seventh in the nation. Three weeks earlier in Detroit, at the USA Outdoor Track and Field Championships, he had finished second to Gunnar Nixon, the number-one-ranked sixteen-year-old high jumper in America. Gunnar jumped six feet seven inches compared to Ryan's six feet five inches, which was the highest Ryan had ever jumped.

Four weeks later the Junior Olympics were held at North Carolina A&T State University in Greensboro. As the event progressed, thirty-five jumpers were eliminated one by one. There were only three left when the bar was raised to six feet seven inches. Each jumper got three attempts to clear that height. This time, however, something was radically different from the meet in Detroit. There was a downpour! But the judges kept the event going. It was raining so hard that the runway was flooded and each step the jumpers took created a splash.

The first jumper was eliminated with a miss on his third jump. Then it was Ryan's turn. He had never jumped that high before, and it was now raining harder than ever. He and Gunnar had both missed their first two attempts. Before Ryan began his run toward the bar, he prayed and was reminded of Philippians 4:13: "I can do *all* things through Christ who strengthens me" (NKJV). Ryan told me that before he started his run, he prayed "4:13" over and over. My wife was back home, and I had her on the phone as our son made his final attempt. Amazingly, he cleared the bar. I found myself choked up by emotion, experiencing an unbelievable level of joy. I shouted to Shannon over the phone, "He did it! He did it! He did it! Our sweet boy is the 2009 *national champion!*"

I don't know if I had ever felt that level of "glory" before that moment. However, a few months later my then fourteen-year-old son, Sean, performed Gershwin's *Rhapsody in Blue,* an eighteen-minute, thirty-one-page concerto. If you know music, you know that this piece is not often even attempted by a teenager. But Sean played it for six hundred people—without a page of music on the piano.

Rhapsody in Blue takes an audience through a range of emotions, and the level of difficulty for the pianist is unimaginable. A number of times the performer has to run the keys in such a way that the hands cross over each other, requiring a level of skill normally seen only in the work of veteran concert pianists.

As I looked around the room, I noticed that tears filled the eyes of countless women and a number of men. When Sean struck the last triumphant chord, cheers erupted, and the audience jumped up to give him a standing ovation. Once again I felt the thrill and glory I had felt two months earlier at Ryan's track-and-field event. I would imagine that you too have had a number of experiences where you felt that kind of glory.

The glory of watching one son compete at the national level and come home with the championship and another son give an amazing performance of a very difficult piano piece was exhilarating. I can't put it into words. I now realize this is the same kind of glory that the Lord wants us to experience when it comes to our relationship with Him. Wouldn't it be wonderful to be this caught up in following the Lord? If that is what God wants for us, then it must be possible. So why don't we experience such all-consuming intimacy with God?

Part of the answer goes back to our understanding of what *faith* and *belief* mean. The consistent experience of glory in our relationship with God does not come from being a casual acquaintance. Nor does it come from involvement in religious activities. It can come only as we experience true intimacy with Him. Real glory can be a *daily* experience as your intimacy with God grows.

It's natural to swell with good feelings when your children excel at something they love: sports, music, friendship, academics, serving others. You have invested in their lives and love them more than you can describe. But with God it's different. How can you have *that* kind of daily, glorious experience with a God you can't see or hear?

The answer is simple. We aren't talking about loving another human or experiencing the glory of seeing a family member do well. We are talking about the promise of an intimate relationship with the Creator of the universe! Everything that exists came into being because God chose to create it. And that's not all. The Creator, in order to save us from our sins, offered His Son to be executed in the cruelest form of capital punishment ever devised. God loves you and me that much!

But God did not send His Son to be the ultimate sacrifice for our sins and then leave us on our own. I know this from personal experience. For forty-seven years He has ordered my life in a way that amazes me—every day. I see His kindness and grace all around. And the more I get to know Him, the more He amazes and astonishes me. The same thing will happen to every person who gets to know God intimately.

You might wonder if I lead an untroubled life that makes it

possible for me to experience such joy and amazement. I do not! Or you might question, "If you had to face my struggles, how could you possibly experience the kind of joy and amazement you're talking about?"

It's a fair question, because God does not smooth out every bump in life. We live in a fallen world, and knowing God intimately does not remove the brokenness and pain that we encounter. If my focus were fixed on the adverse circumstances, setbacks, and obstacles of life, I would forfeit the glory of my relationship with God. But even in the midst of frustration and fatigue, confusion and loss, when I shift my focus away from myself to Christ, my heart is instantly filled with amazement, gratitude, and joy. I have seen others who, although they were in pain beyond description, fixed their hearts on the Lord Jesus and experienced the same kind of liberation and transformation.

Imagine that you were in the worst circumstances of your life—so trying that you wondered how you could make it through another hour. Then suddenly Jesus appeared. At that moment would you still be thinking about your circumstances, or would you stand in awe of Christ? Now imagine that He put His arms around you and gently said, "My sweet child, do not let your heart be troubled. Trust in God; trust also in Me. In My Father's house are many rooms; if it were not so, I would have told you. I am going there to prepare a place for you. And if I go and prepare a place for you, I will come back and take you to be with Me that you also may be where I am" (see John 14:1–3). Imagine that He went on to say, "In this world you will have trouble. But take heart! I have overcome the world" (John 16:33). And then He said to you, "Therefore I tell you, do not worry about your life, what you will eat or drink; or about your body, what you will wear.... Therefore do not worry about tomorrow" (Matthew 6:25, 34).

And looking into your eyes, He closed by saying, "From now on, anytime you are weary, troubled, or stressed out in any way, come to Me! I'll carry your load. Tie yourself to Me, and learn from Me! I promise, I'll do the work and lighten your load!" (see Matthew 11:28–30). And then, as quickly as He came, He left.

Would you still be focused on your horrible circumstances, or would your heart be pounding with joy, excitement, and new-found peace? No matter what your circumstances may be, when you *truly* know Christ, then His words and presence fill your vision, relieve your stress, and crowd out your fears and unbelief.

Jesus has said the words I paraphrased above, and He addresses them to you. As you come to know Him and all that He said to you, everything in your life will change!

KNOWING GOD IS LOVING GOD

In 1970 I attended the Campus Crusade for Christ's Institute of Biblical Studies. One of the professors was Dr. Manford Gutzke, an incredible Bible teacher. Every day he taught us wondrous lessons from the Bible, and every day he would close our class with this statement: "To *know* Him is to *love* Him. If you don't love Him, if you don't adore Him, it's because you simply do *not* know Him." At the time I wondered why Dr. Gutzke kept harping on this statement. I knew Christ at the time, but I also knew I did not have the kind of adoration for Him that Dr. Gutzke had.

All these years later I finally understand what he was talking about. Though I knew all about Jesus and God the Father, I really didn't *know* either one of them. During the past few years, I *have* come to know Him—and now I agree that to *know* Him is to love Him, adore Him, and stand in awe of Him.

I want you to know these things as well. I want you to be equipped with everything you need to come to know Christ intimately so that you develop a relationship that goes deeper day by day, month by month, and year after year.

From Jeremiah to Jesus

Intimately knowing God is not just an Old Testament concept proclaimed by God to Israel through the prophet Jeremiah. Fast-forward 650 years to Jesus, just a few hours before His crucifixion. He was in the upper room with His disciples, praying to His Father. Here, Jesus went one giant step further than God had proclaimed to Jeremiah. He not only confirmed that intimacy is God's desire for us; He said that intimacy with the Father and Son is the *essence* of *eternal life*! Jesus said, "And this is eternal life, that they may *know* You, the only true God, and Jesus Christ whom You have sent" (John 17:3, NKJV).

Jesus used the Greek word that means to "know intimately." This statement is life changing in two ways. First, it reveals that intimacy with the Father and Son is what eternal life is all about. And beyond that, it shows that eternal life is not something that we experience only after we die. It begins during *this* life!

Here is one more fact to consider. Not only is our intimacy with God the desire of God's heart and the essence of eternal life, but it is the irrefutable evidence that we are truly born again. Remember Jesus' final terrifying declaration to some people who claimed to know Him? He said, "Depart from Me" (Matthew 7:23, NKJV). Why did people who were convinced they were followers of Christ come up short? It wasn't because they didn't believe in Christ in their minds. Remember, they had performed miracles in His name. These were devoted, religious people.

Still, Jesus' condemning pronouncement was based on the only criterion that God says defines faith, and that is knowing God intimately. Jesus declared, "I never *knew* you" (Matthew 7:23). He was speaking to people who had called Him *Lord.* He didn't deny that they had performed miracles in His name. But He made it clear that they were people He did not know. Of course, He knew all about them. He knew their thoughts, motives, and intentions. But He did not intimately know them. He was not connected to them the way an adoring husband is connected to his loving wife.

Does Christ Know You?

What are we to conclude about religious people who performed miracles in Jesus' name but whose faith was declared invalid? It goes back to what was in their hearts. And what was in their hearts was evidenced by their behavior, which Jesus characterized as "lawlessness" (see Matthew 7:23, NASB).

You can claim to know Christ, but the critical question is, does *He* know *you*? Are you intimately connected to Him? Do you love what He loves and hate what He hates? Are His values your values? Or is your life characterized by self-centered behavior that makes *you* the god of your life? Are God's laws something you call to mind and then dismiss as you choose to follow your own agenda? If that is the pattern of your life, then you may hear the terrible words "I never knew you" when you come face to face with Christ. That is the bad news I mentioned previously.

But there is good news, and it is the greatest news on earth. The great news is that everything can change the moment you are born again. But as we go back to Christ's words and teachings, being born again might mean something quite different from what you think it does.

So the answer to the question "What does God want from me?" is simple. He wants you to enter into an intimate relationship with Him and His Son. And that leads to the second question: "How can I enter into the type of intimacy that God desires?" The answer to that question might surprise you. As you will see in the next chapter, to live in intimacy with God means that you must love Him the way *He* wants to be loved. And His "love language" is far different from ours.

CHAPTER 4

How to Love God the Way *He* Wants to Be Loved

Intimacy means different things to different people. The question to answer is, what does it mean to God?

O ne day in 1991, shortly before my wedding to Shannon, author and relationship-expert Gary Smalley taught me a crucial lesson about intimacy. It was simple yet profound. He said, "If a man wants true intimacy with his wife, it's not *his* definition of intimacy that's important. It's *hers*. She alone holds the key to her heart, so she is the one who decides when and how to give it away!"

He added, "And if a woman wants intimacy with a man, it's not her definition that's important. It's his. For he alone holds the key to his heart and is the only one who decides when and how to give it."

This is simple enough to understand, but it's not easy. And

here's why. What a woman desires and requires for intimacy is quite different from what a man desires and requires. Intimacy does not mean the same thing to both spouses.

The same is true with God. If we want to experience intimacy with Him, the important thing is not how you or I define an intimate relationship. What matters is how God defines it. Thankfully, Jesus didn't leave us clueless. On this subject He gave us a crystal-clear definition.

At the Last Supper, Jesus gave His disciples some of the most important instructions they would ever receive. He was telling them how they could have true intimacy with Him even after He was no longer physically present on earth. He explained that He would send the Holy Spirit to be with them, to be their Teacher and Counselor, and to live within them. Christ also explained that the disciples would "bear much fruit" as a result of their intimacy with Him (John 15:8).

It was here that Jesus defined intimacy with God. In John 14:21, He said, "He who has My commandments and keeps them, it is *he* who loves Me. And he who loves Me will be loved by My Father, and I will love him and manifest [reveal or disclose] Myself to him" (NKJV). In this simple statement Jesus reveals four amazing truths. Each one is not only applicable to life on earth but also to eternity in heaven.

First, He reveals God's definition of intimacy, showing exactly how we can love the Father and Son in the way *they* want to be loved! The way Christ wants to be loved is for us to hear His commands and obey them. He reveals that we love Him, not with emotions and feelings that we normally associate with love, but by *obedience* to Him. He said, "If you love me, you will obey what I command" (John 14:15).

He didn't end His explanation here. He gave us three more truths. The second eternal truth is that when we love Him through obedience, we will be loved by the Father in a special way. Those who follow Christ's commands become the object and focus of God's special love.

The third and fourth eternal truths go hand in hand. Just like the Father, Jesus also will love us in a special way—a way that reflects the highest level of intimacy. He said He will "manifest" Himself to us. He will reveal to us His deepest feelings, His highest values and priorities. He will reveal to us what He loves and what He hates. He will reveal His heart in ways that are not available to those who are not intimate with Him.

The Greek word that is translated "manifest" in John 14:21 is the word *emphanizo* and is broader in scope than just imparting knowledge. It implies an obvious manifestation. That is, He will make His presence known to you, and He will open His heart to you. You will see Him in a way that others don't. You will experience all that He is in a tangible way that is hidden from those who don't love Him by obeying His commands. If you will take God seriously enough to discover Jesus' teachings and commands and practice them, you will experience deep intimacy with the infinite God of the universe.

And there is even more to the third promise. Jesus said, "If anyone loves me, he will obey my teaching. My Father will love him, and we will come to him and make our home with him. He who does not love me will not obey my teaching. These words you hear are not my own; they belong to the Father who sent me" (John 14:23–24).

Here, Jesus clarified and expanded on what He said in John 14:21. In verse 21, He said that we love Him by keeping His commands. Here He replaced the word *commands* with a broader word that literally means "words" or "teaching." So we love Him not only by obeying His commands but also by obeying His *teachings*. We are to give the same weight to His instructions and admonitions for our lives that we would give a clearly stated command.

It's important to realize that Christ is *not* saying we obey His commands to gain eternal life. Salvation is a matter of God's grace and our faith. But obedience is essential, because it is the way to express our love for Him in the way He wants to be loved. And when we do this, He makes one more amazing promise. He says that He and the Father will come to us and literally make their home with us. Unbelievable. How would you like to have God the Father and the Lord Jesus Christ living in your home—available to you twenty-four hours a day, seven days a week? That is what He is offering.

And finally, Jesus draws one more line in the sand to make sure there is no confusion about the way He wants to be loved. He says, "He who does not love me will not obey my teaching" (John 14:24). This statement could not be any clearer: If you obey Christ's teachings, you love Him. And if you *don't* obey His teachings, you don't love Him! In John 15:14, Jesus says, "You are my friends if you do what I command." And in Matthew 12:50, He says those who *do* the will of His Father are members of His family. What could be better than to be the friend and brother of Jesus Christ?

A LIBERATING AND EXHILARATING TRUTH

As I began to understand the incredible truths of John 14:15, 21, 23–24, it was as if a thousand-pound weight were being lifted off my shoulders. As far back as I can remember, one sentence from

Jesus' lips had always bothered me. He said, "Anyone who loves his father or mother more than me is not worthy of me; anyone who loves his son or daughter more than me is not worthy of me" (Matthew 10:37).

Every time I read those words, I felt a terrible weight of guilt and inadequacy. As I compared my feelings for my family to my feelings for the Lord, it seemed there was no way that I could love Jesus as much as I loved my mom and dad, my wife, and my children. I told Him over and over again, "Lord, You know the truth. My love for my family seems so much greater than my love for You, and I don't know what to do about it." It seemed as if there was no way out—no way I could love Him more than I loved my own family.

But I was making a terrible mistake! I was measuring my love for Him by the same standard I've always used to measure my love for my family—by my *feelings* of love. Most of the time my feelings of love for my family towered over my feelings of love for Christ. But His words in John 14 changed everything! Jesus made it clear that we love Him not with feelings but with actions. That made all the difference for me. By doing what He tells me to do, by obeying His commands and instructions for my life, I love Christ. What a difference.

My feelings have not changed toward my family, but using Christ's definition, I *do* love Him more than my wife and children. When I sense He wants me to do something that conflicts with my desire to be with my family, He wins more and more often. When I hear His call to go somewhere that will cause me to be apart from my family, I usually go. I am choosing His will over my will, and in doing that I am loving Him more than I am loving my family.

I know Christ wants me to love my wife the way He loves His followers, which is sacrificially (see Ephesians 5:25). I know He wants me to love my children in ways that will show them that no other person loves them more than Dad does. And there are countless times that obeying Jesus means loving my family *more* and in better ways than my nature would otherwise push me to do. If I'm angry with my wife or children, He commands me to instantly forgive and turn the other cheek, even if I don't feel like it. When I obey those commands, I am loving Him by loving my family. I wish I had discovered these truths forty years ago.

And here's the icing on the cake: the more I focus on loving Him by obeying His teachings, the more my *feelings* for Him grow. There are times of worship and times of meditating on Christ's words when my feelings toward Him soar to new heights. And why should we expect anything else? As He fulfills His promise to reveal Himself to us, we see Him as He really is, and our passion for Him is ignited.

Are you starting to see the power of these revelations from the Lord Jesus? Loving God by obeying His teachings and commands is not easy, but it removes all confusion over what it takes to love the Lord. In God's eyes, obeying Him from our hearts equals loving Him. However, this leads to a crucial question: how can we ever know and keep His commands?

I mentioned earlier that I spent two years organizing all of Jesus' statements into topics. One of those topics is the "Commands of Christ." These are all the stated and implied commands that He gave to His followers. As I studied His commands, I was amazed by the incredible power they give anyone who is committed to following Him. By studying the red words in the New Testament, you can learn His commands, and empowered by the

Holy Spirit, you can live your life according to what Christ wants for you and from you.

DON'T CONFUSE HIS COMMANDS WITH THE MORAL LAW

One day I asked the pastor of a large church, "How many commands do you think Jesus gave to His followers?" He said, "Well, we all know the big three." He rattled off, "'You shall love the LORD your God with all your heart, with all your soul, with all your mind, and with all your strength.' 'You shall love your neighbor as yourself,' and 'A new commandment I give to you, that you love one another; as I have loved you'" (Mark 12:30–31; John 13:34, NKJV).

I said, "Well, you got one right. The first two you mentioned were commandments from the *moral law,* and the moral law was given for a different purpose than were the commands of Christ. The third was indeed one of Jesus' commands, so you were right on that one."

Then I asked, "Do you know the other one hundred forty commands that Jesus gave His followers?" The pastor's head dropped as he said, "Ugh, I can't even do the 'big ten.' I can't imagine doing one hundred forty-one."

I told him, "No, you don't get it. *No one* can do the 'big ten.' The Pharisees *thought* they could keep the moral law, but then Jesus revealed the spirit of the Law in the Sermon on the Mount and made it clear that no one could keep the law for even a day." Can anyone honestly say, "Today I did it. I loved the Lord with *all* my heart, *all* my mind, *all* my soul, and *all* my strength"? Absolutely not. Can anyone say, "Today I did it… I loved my neighbor as myself"? Most of the time, we can't even love our spouses the way we love ourselves, much less our neighbors. And Jesus went even further when He said that if you lust after a woman, you have committed adultery. And if you have been angry at your brother, you've committed murder. To this our response can only be, "God, be merciful to me, a sinner!"

The moral law was given to reveal God's perfect righteousness and our spiritual bankruptcy. With God, there's no hint of un-righteousness, while, by comparison, every strand of our human-nature DNA is stained by self-centeredness and sinful intentions and motives. As Isaiah wrote, "And all our righteousnesses are like filthy rags" when compared to God's righteousness (Isaiah 64:6, NKJV). Paul describes us in Ephesians as being "dead in trespasses and sins" and "having no hope" (Ephesians 2:1, 12, NKJV). We were all found guilty and sentenced to death under God's moral law, which is why we need the sacrifice of His Son to pay for our sin. Paul said the purpose of the Law was to tutor us, to bring us to Christ so we can be justified by faith (see Galatians 3:24; Romans 5:1). Once the Law delivered us to Christ and to faith, Paul said, it was no longer needed (see Galatians 3:24–25). But this is *not* the case with the commands of Jesus, which serve entirely different purposes.

THREE PURPOSES OF JESUS' COMMANDS

Jesus' commands are not designed to convince us that we are sin-ners separated from a holy God. His commands do a very differ-ent work, when we understand their purposes. The three purposes are (1) to reveal unseen truths that have been hidden by darkness,

(2) to reveal God's will for every moment of our days, and (3) to empower us with the grace we need to live according to God's will in every circumstance.

1. To Reveal Unseen Truths Hidden by Darkness

I grew up in Phoenix, Arizona, where I was part of a Boy Scout troop. When I was eleven, our troop went camping in the mountains just south of the city. That night an overcast sky blocked all light from the moon and the stars. It was so dark I couldn't see anything that was one foot in front of me. While walking with some friends, I got separated from my buddy who had a flashlight. That's when a "jumping cactus" embedded itself in my leg. I jumped to the side in pain and landed on a rock, twisting an ankle. I was hurting and in complete darkness, and for a few minutes I stayed completely still. Just then a friend pointed his flashlight in my direction. I had stopped just inches from a high ledge. But thanks to my friend and the light from his flashlight, I was safe. With the benefit of light, I could navigate the path back to our tent, where we pulled cactus spines out of my leg.

Jesus said, "I am the light of the world. Whoever follows me will never walk in darkness, but will have the light of life" (John 8:12). Unlike His first followers, you and I can't follow Jesus physically. The only way we can follow Him is to learn His instructions and commands and then do them. Jesus' commands are like a one-million-watt spotlight shining into a dark desert night. They reveal the landscape around us, which we would otherwise be blind to. The light of Jesus' commands keeps us from falling off spiritual cliffs. The light of His commands makes us aware of the danger and hidden threats that we are about to stumble into.

His words uncover the *realities* of life and show us God's eternal values. The contrast between Jesus' commands and the deadly illusions of the world is dramatic and life changing.

When we live in darkness, it's easy to fall into a trap. It could be chasing wealth and focusing on acquiring things, or seeking status and success regardless of what they may cost us. But Jesus commands us to "Be on your guard against all kinds of greed." He tells us, "A man's life does not consist in the abundance of his possessions" (Luke 12:15). The world contradicts the commands of the Lord. It tells us that chasing wealth and acquiring lots of things are the best parts of life—a bigger home, a newer car, a better flat-screen television, and a bigger bank account. Those are the things that are supposed to deliver all the happiness we long for.

With only one command, Jesus turns on the light. He warns us to be on guard against all kinds of greed. His light reveals that our lives really *aren't* defined by material possessions or return on investment. Then He lights up even more landscape, revealing the path to avoid. "Do not store up for yourselves treasures on earth." He next shines His light on the path we should follow: "Store up for yourselves treasures in heaven" that won't be destroyed or diminished with the passing of time. And here is the reason: "For where your treasure is, there your heart will be also" (Matthew 6:19–21).

With two commands He illuminated the world's path, which results in a life that is wasted for eternity. However, He then showed us the path that makes our lives *count* for eternity. As we follow Jesus by embracing His commands, His promise is fulfilled: we will not walk in darkness; we will have "the light of life" (John 8:12).

2. To Reveal God's Miraculous Will for Us in Every Moment

Second, Christ's commands reveal the awesome will of God for us, not in broad strokes or generalities, but in great detail, moment by moment. We don't have to guess what His will might be in any given situation.

In college I met a guy who was planning to dive in the darkness. He was on the university's diving team. One day a Christian told him about God's love and about Jesus dying on the cross in his place. The diving-team member gave it a lot of thought but didn't commit his life to Christ. That night he decided to go to the school's indoor pool, alone, and get in a few dives.

The pool area was pitch black, and the diver couldn't turn on the lights, because it was against the rules to be in the pool after hours. He climbed to a diving platform, walked to the edge, and raised his arms from his side. Just then a sliver of moonlight shone through a window behind him. He saw his shadow cast on the opposite wall. It was a silhouette that looked like a man hanging on a cross. As he gazed at the sight, he remembered what he had heard earlier about Jesus dying on the cross for his sins.

The weight of what Jesus had done began to fill his heart and mind. He remembered that Jesus said, "Come unto me" (Matthew 11:28, KJV). Then he sat on the platform and began to pray. He said later that he responded to Christ's command to come to Him. The diver committed his life to the Savior and was overcome with emotion. No longer wanting to take any practice dives, he climbed down from the platform.

As he walked to an exit, a janitor came in through another entrance and turned on the lights. The diver looked back and could not believe what he saw. The pool had been drained that day. If he had taken a practice jump, it would have been his last. His life was saved by light coming through a window, by a shadow that symbolized Christ on the cross, and by God's light in a command of Christ for that precise moment in his life: "Come unto me."

3. To Empower Us with the Grace to Do His Will in Every Circumstance

The third role of Christ's commands is that of empowering us. They not only provide direction; they provide the means by which we can walk by faith and please God. They are like fuel that empowers us to do God's will. And behind all this is God's grace, the ultimate power source that gives us the desire to discover and do God's will (see Philippians 2:13).

When Peter saw Jesus walking on water, at first he and the other disciples in the boat were terrified because they thought they were seeing a ghost. Then Peter realized it was Jesus, and he was gripped by a desire to do the impossible—to walk on water. But first he needed a command from the Lord that would make the impossible possible. Peter needed a command that his faith and feet could step out on.

He said, "Lord, if it is You, command me to come to You on the water." With a single word, Jesus gave him what he needed. Jesus commanded, "Come" (Matthew 14:28–29, NKJV). With that, Peter stepped out in faith and became the only other man in history to walk on water.

And that was done in response to just *one* word. Consider that Christ has given us more than one hundred commands, and He invites us to step out in faith on each one.

Moral Law in Contrast to Christ's Commands

It's unfortunate that so many view Christ's commands as a weight or burden or limitation on the way they live. This is a lie that keeps them from the joy of obedience. Speaking of the commands of Christ, the apostle John wrote, "This is love for God: to obey his commands. And his commands are not burdensome" (1 John 5:3). The commands that Christ gave us are God's love language. The moral law shows us we are sinners, falling short of God's righteousness. But Christ's commands free us and show us how to live.

In my book *The Greatest Words Ever Spoken*, the words of Jesus are organized by subject and then into specific topics. In just one of the topics, the "Commands of Christ," we find one hundred forty-one stated and implied commands. The first two listed are found in John 4:35: "Do you not say, 'Four months more and then the harvest'? I tell you, open your eyes and look at the fields! They are ripe for harvest." Jesus tells us to (1) stop procrastinating and (2) come into the reality of each moment—open our eyes and see the fields in front of us, ready for harvesting. Every day God brings people into your path, and He wants you to see them as white fields ripe for harvest. You are to be Christ's ears, arms, and voice to them. If they need to be heard, listen. If they need to be encouraged or comforted, give them a hug or an uplifting word. If they need to hear the words of Jesus, be His voice.

Is that a burdensome command? Not at all! And as we saw with the diving-team member, Jesus' command in Matthew 11:28–29 is not burdensome. It is comforting! He tells us, "Come to me, all you who are weary and burdened, and I will give you rest. Take my yoke upon you and learn from me, for I am gentle and humble in heart, and you will find rest for your souls." Whenever we are fearful, stressed, or spent, we are to go straight to Him. And not just for a counseling visit but so that we might harness ourselves to Him.

He tells us to *learn* from Him and then adds two amazing promises. First, He will give rest to our souls in a way that no one else can. Second, *He* will lighten our burden and carry the weight of our load. Oh what a Savior!

The apostle John said, "We love Him because He first loved us" (1 John 4:19, NKJV). With every command and promise Jesus gives, we see His amazing love in a new way. And by discovering and doing what Christ taught, *we* can love Him and God the Father using Their love language—the way They want to be loved. If that doesn't get you excited, set this book aside and get on your knees. Ask Christ to open the eyes of your soul, then reread this chapter. (Also, if you don't already have it, get a copy of *The Greatest Words Ever Spoken,* thin-line edition. It will help you refer to the words of Christ throughout the day and will be a tool for loving God like few others in your toolbox.)

THE ROCK-SOLID FOUNDATION FOR YOUR LIFE

In Matthew 7:24–27, Jesus says your life will be built on one of two foundations (there are no other options). One foundation is rock, which enables you to overcome all the trials of this world. It is the evidence of new birth and your saving faith. The other foundation is sand, and anyone who builds on it will see their "faith" *collapse* in the storms of life. This is the kind of outward religious faith that will invite the dreaded words of Jesus: "I never knew you; depart from me, you who practice lawlessness" (Matthew 7:23, NASB).

But how do we know false faith from true, saving faith? In verses 24 and 25, Jesus said, "Therefore whoever hears these sayings of Mine, and *does* them, I will liken him to a wise man who built his house on the rock: and the rain descended, the floods came, and the winds blew and beat on that house; and it did not fall, for it was founded on the rock." And in verses 26 and 27, He said, "But everyone who hears these sayings of Mine, and does not do them, will be like a foolish man who built his house on the sand: and the rain descended, the floods came, and the winds blew and beat on that house; and it fell. And great was its fall" (NKJV).

The solid foundation of rock is defined as hearing Jesus' words or teachings and doing them. The shifting foundation of sand gives way under those who hear His teachings but *fail* to do them.

Does that mean that eternal life is based on your obedience? If you fail to do what Christ commanded, will you be lost? Absolutely not! You receive eternal life when you are truly born again. But the only true evidence of new birth is that you build your life, your attitudes, and your behavior on the rock of *hearing and doing* what He said. And as you're about to see in the next chapter, being born again may be radically different from what you have been taught.

CHAPTER 5

BEING BORN AGAIN IS NOT WHAT MOST OF US THINK

Are you ready to risk your eternal destiny on your *definition?*

On September 11, 2001, a friend of mine, Jason H., was starting his workday on the 104th floor of the south tower (Two World Trade Center). That is when he heard what he describes as a big *whoosh.* He went to a window and, to his horror, saw a giant hole in the north tower. Smoke and flames were pouring out. It was such a surreal sight that for a minute it was almost as if he were hypnotized by it. Then he felt a tug on his arm. "Mr. H.," his assistant said, "we have to get out of here. Come on, we have to go."

They headed to a stairwell and began the long trip down dozens of flights of stairs. When they arrived at the 78th floor, they had to exit the stairwell, cross the sky lobby, and use a different stairwell to continue down to the ground floor. As they walked across the lobby, they heard a series of announcements coming over the PA system. A voice informed them, "This building is secure. Please return to your offices immediately. The explosion in Tower One was an isolated event. There is *no* danger to this building."

Jason's assistant started to walk to the bank of elevators to head back to their floor. But Jason didn't believe the building was safe; he didn't feel right about going back to the 104th floor. It was as if a voice were warning him, "Get out of the building as fast as you can." He told his assistant that he didn't believe it was safe and that he planned to keep going down. He urged her to come with him. But as her company's designated fire marshal, she had been trained what to do when the Port Authority announced an all clear. She was confident that the authorities would issue the all clear only when they *knew* there was no danger. To avoid panic and the possibility of injury, fire marshals had been directed to tell workers to return to their offices.

As Jason walked toward the entrance to the stairwell to the ground level, his assistant and most of the other employees of his company gathered at the elevators to head back to their offices. The prospect of hurrying down seventy-eight floors was not something he was looking forward to, because he was overweight and out of shape. But he couldn't ignore the little voice in his head. As he entered the stairwell, he glanced back at his assistant and his other friends waiting for an elevator. He had to ask himself who was making the right choice. Was the danger he sensed real? Was the long, exhausting journey to the ground floor the right choice or a waste of time and effort?

All second-guessing came to an abrupt end moments later. Jason had made it down only one floor when he heard and felt a terrible explosion. The impact was so violent that it felt as if the tower swayed down to the ground and then sprang back up. Everyone in the stairway was thrown down. But as fast as they could, they resumed their long trip down. What Jason didn't know was that a wing of the second jet had cut through the 78th floor, causing an explosion and instantly killing his friends as they waited for elevators to go back to their offices.

Once on the ground, Jason felt he had to run as fast as he could to get far away from the building. The voice told him to keep running, and so he did. Even though he was out of breath and approaching the point of exhaustion, he kept running. Then behind him he heard a terrible grinding noise as the building began to collapse. After questioning the Port Authority's instructions, Jason had survived the worst day of his life.

THE DANGER OF TRUSTING
THE WRONG AUTHORITY

The tragedy is that Jason's friends and co-workers did *exactly* what their trusted authorities had told them to do. And the authorities were acting in good faith, based on the information available to them. They announced what they sincerely believed to be the truth. But as sincere as everyone was, they all were sincerely wrong. The problem many of us run into is that the authorities we trust may not know the *whole* truth.

This same tragedy is being repeated with millions of sincere church members and professing Christians—but with infinitely worse consequences. People who followed the Port Authority's instructions paid a terrible price for their misplaced faith. But an even more terrible price will be paid by millions who blindly entrust their eternal destiny to the guidance of many sincere religious leaders. These religious teachers and pastors continue to teach that there is an accepted formula for receiving eternal life. However, Jesus did not give us a formula. These leaders are as sure of their traditional teachings as the Port Authority was convinced that the south tower was safe on September 11, 2001. And yet, when the directives of religious leaders are compared to the statements of Jesus, many fall short. And those who follow such directives are in terrible danger of hearing Christ tell them He never knew them.

That's the bad news. The good news is that it doesn't have to be that way. As we have seen, in the verses that immediately follow Jesus' terrifying warning, He revealed that there is a rock-solid foundation upon which a person's faith can safely rest (see Matthew 7:24–25). On September 11, 2001, there were only two paths that Jason and his co-workers could take—one led to safety and life, the other to death. The same is true with eternal life. Jesus says there are two paths a person can take. One path leads to life, the other to death. One creates a life that will withstand all the storms of life and judgment at the end of our earthly life. The other produces a life that will be forever altered, in a terrible way, by those same storms.

Jesus Is the Ultimate Authority on Eternal Life

The problem with the Port Authority's announcement on September 11, 2001, was the decision makers didn't have all the information. They could only guess at the future, and they guessed wrong. Not so with Jesus. He *alone* has a perfect understanding of how to enter the kingdom of God, because He alone came down from heaven to reveal what He and God the Father *know* to be the truth (see John 3:10–13; 6:38–40). When it comes to the future and the truth about eternal life, Jesus did not teach what He hoped was true.

Unlike all others who claim to be authorities, Jesus stated what He *knew*. His words alone are the standard, the authority, and the judge by which everyone will be measured (see John 12:48).

Jesus explained that everything He said was *exactly* what the Father commanded Him to say. The Father even commanded Him how to say it (see John 12:48–50). It doesn't matter what anyone else teaches about gaining eternal life. No other teacher has Christ's qualifications. None of us came from heaven to earth with the truth about eternal life. But Jesus did! So as we consider what Jesus said about being born again, I hope you will realize that He is the only Authority whose words should shape your belief and behavior. If we add anything to what He taught or take anything away from it, we alter His perfect message. And if we alter that perfect message, then we pervert the truth and lead ourselves, our families, and anyone who trusts our word down the broad path to destruction (see Matthew 7:13).

How Jesus Defines "Born Again"

Under the cover of darkness, a rich Jewish ruler approached Jesus. He was a member of the strictest sect of Jewish religious leaders, and he asked Jesus the most important question any of us will ever have. The question on Nicodemus's mind was, what must a person do to become a part of God's eternal kingdom and receive eternal life? (See John 3.)

While he didn't approach Jesus in public, he came with the utmost sincerity. Nicodemus began by stating what he believed to be true about Jesus: "Rabbi, we know that You are a teacher come from God; for no one can do these signs that You do unless God is with him" (John 3:2, NKJV).

Jesus didn't get bogged down with polite chitchat. Instead, He answered the question that weighed on Nicodemus's heart. "I tell you the truth, no one can see the kingdom of God unless he is born again" (verse 3). Not understanding this answer, Nicodemus asked, "How can a man be born when he is old? Surely he cannot enter a second time into his mother's womb to be born!" (verse 4).

Jesus answered, "I tell you the truth, no one can enter the kingdom of God unless he is born of water and the Spirit. Flesh gives birth to flesh, but the Spirit gives birth to spirit. You should not be surprised at my saying, 'You must be born again'" (verses 5–7).

The expression "born of water" referred to physical birth, bringing to mind the breaking of the amniotic sac, which initiates physical birth. Jesus was explaining that in addition to one's physical birth, there must be a second birth that is spiritual. Without the second birth, no one can enter God's kingdom. Further, while the sources of a physical birth are human parents, the source of the spiritual birth is the Spirit of God—the Holy Spirit. But according to Jesus and the apostle John, there is one additional difference between a physical birth and a spiritual birth. A physical birth is initiated by the human will. A man and woman choose to be physically intimate, and the birth of a child follows. But a spiritual birth is *not* a mere act of the human will. Spiritual birth is initiated solely by God, independent of a person's will or impulse (see John 1:12–13). And since it is an act of God, exactly when it happens can't be calculated by anyone on earth. However, when a spiritual birth does take place, it creates an effect and produces evidence that *can* be seen by others. Jesus explained it to Nicodemus like this: "The wind blows wherever it pleases. You hear its sound, but you cannot tell where it comes from or where it is going. So it is with everyone born of the Spirit" (John 3:8).

Jesus went on to explain that God's love for us is so great that God *gave* His one and only Son, that whoever would believe *in Him* would have eternal life (see John 3:16).

And as we saw in chapter 3, belief is not merely intellectual agreement or acceptance. It refers to an attitude of full trust and commitment. In summary, here is what Jesus teaches about eternal life.

JESUS' DESCRIPTION OF ENTERING GOD'S KINGDOM AND GAINING ETERNAL LIFE

Jesus explained that the second birth is necessary and pointed out the evidence of that birth that is specific to being born again.

1. You must have a *second* birth (see John 3:3, 5).
   a. That birth is a *spiritual* birth (see John 3:5–6).
   b. That birth is initiated by the Holy Spirit, not something you come up with on your own (see John 1:13; 3:5–6).
2. When the second birth takes place, there is specific evidence. The evidence is *receiving* and *believing* Jesus and His words (see John 1:12).
   a. Receiving and believing Him and His words produce a total commitment to Him and a trust or reliance on Him and His Word (see John 3:16–21).
      (1) That trust and commitment produce a desire and power to hear and do what Jesus taught and commanded (see John 3:21; Matthew 7:24; John 10:27–28).

       (a) *Hearing* and *doing* what Jesus said result in choices and behaviors that build a life that reflects and demonstrates the teachings of the Lord (see Matthew 7:24–25).

       (b) That life will endure all the storms of life and the judgment we all will face.

If Jesus' teachings on being born again were diagrammed, they would look like this:

The Holy Spirit (gives) ⇨ spiritual birth (resulting in) ⇨ eternal life (which is evidenced by) ⇨ repentance and faith in Christ (producing) ⇨ the desire and power to do what Jesus said to do (building) ⇨ a life that withstands the storms of living and ultimately the judgment.

WHY IS A NEW BIRTH NECESSARY?

Jesus went on to reveal to Nicodemus *why* a person has to be born again. In John 3:19, He said, "This is the verdict: Light has come into the world, but men loved darkness instead of light because their deeds were evil." Ever since Adam's fall, human nature has been to love ourselves more than we love God or other people. Simply stated, our nature is to sin—to do that which falls woefully short of God's standards.

It's always possible to find someone else who seems to fall far shorter of the mark than we do, making us feel superior by comparison. But when we compare ourselves to *God's* standards, even our best efforts are woefully inadequate. As we saw earlier, Jesus said if we have been angry with someone, by God's standard we've committed murder in our hearts. If we have lusted after someone, we have committed adultery in our hearts (see Matthew

5:21–28). God is so holy and righteous that breaking the *spirit* of His law is as bad as breaking the *letter* of that law. The apostle Paul stated it this way: "For all have sinned and fall short of the glory of God" (Romans 3:23, NKJV). He also said, "For the wages of sin is death" (Romans 6:23, NKJV). He wrote that every person begins life "dead in trespasses and sins" (Ephesians 2:1, NKJV).

Because sin killed our spirits and changed our nature, it is impossible for us to generate, on our own, any desire for a holy and righteous God. Though we would all be attracted to a Santa Claus God who exists only to love us and never to condemn us, that is not the one true God. The same God who delights in exercising love and mercy also exercises judgment and righteousness (see Jeremiah 9:24). And that is *not* the kind of God a human is naturally attracted to.

Jesus explained this aspect of human nature: "Everyone who does evil hates the light, and will not come into the light for fear that his deeds will be exposed" (John 3:20). Putting together everything Jesus and Paul said, we can see that our only hope for eternal life and intimacy with God is to receive a brand-new nature—one that is alive to God. That is the nature that will lead us to love Him the way He wants to be loved.

Jesus made it clear that being born again is a requirement, but it is not something we can initiate. Since God is the One who acts by His Spirit to bring about the second birth, what can we do to make sure we have been born again?

CHAPTER 6

HOW TO *KNOW* YOU
ARE BORN AGAIN

*Fact: Jesus said you cannot enter the
kingdom of God unless you are born again.*

*Fact: This second birth is performed by
the Spirit of God. You can't be born
again through an act of your will.*

*Fact: The effects of the second birth
are easily seen by others.*

I t's not easy to avoid formulas. Dieters use them to determine the caloric content of breakfast, lunch, and dinner. Financial advisors rely on them to help clients set up a household budget and determine amounts for savings, investments, and a reasonable car payment or mortgage.

Formulas have their place, but when it comes to eternal life, our tendency to fall back on formulas has steered untold numbers of people wrong. When Jesus answered Nicodemus's questions about being born again, He did not rely on a formula. The same is not true, however, when Christians today talk about how we can receive eternal life. The statements that Jesus and the apostle John made about the new birth (in John 1 and 3) reveal the misrepresentations of the gospel that have been promoted by modern evangelical formulas.

Well-meaning Christians often teach that praying a certain prayer or walking down a church aisle and "accepting Christ" produces a born-again event that makes a person a Christian. But Jesus, when asked directly about eternal life, said nothing of the sort. I am not saying that evangelicals should abandon altar calls, but we should make sure that our message accurately conveys what Jesus actually taught rather than what evangelical tradition has formulated.

Different denominations and Christian traditions convey their distinctive formulas for becoming a Christian. Some say:

- Eternal life is secured by joining a church and being baptized.
- Pray a prayer of repentance of sin, include a confession of faith in Christ and His work on the cross, and then receive Christ by asking Him to come into your heart.
- You need all the above, *plus* you have to live a worthy life, and then you have a good chance of gaining eternal life.

Tens of millions have joined churches, been baptized, prayed prayers of repentance, confessed their faith in Christ, and asked Him to come into their lives. Of those tens of millions, many really have been born again and built their lives, choices, and actions on the teachings of the Lord Jesus Christ. But for those who were born again, their new birth did not *result* from being baptized, praying a prayer, or receiving Christ into their hearts. Rather, it resulted from the fact that God gave life to their dead spirits through His Spirit.

The formulaic teachings have it backward. Asking to be baptized or praying a prayer of repentance doesn't produce the new birth. Rather, they may be *evidence* of a new birth. Most of the supporting scriptures that are used to defend a certain prayer, a public profession of faith, or baptism as a means to obtain eternal life are taken out of context. They are broadened to apply to something beyond what their context specifies.

When I speak of context, I'm not talking about only the context of the verse itself, meaning the paragraphs surrounding the verse. I'm talking about the context of the *whole* of Christ's teaching on the subject. Contemporary definitions of such words as *confess, believe,* and *receive* are very different from the corresponding words of Jesus recorded by the writers of the New Testament.

We've already looked at the radical difference between the meaning of the ancient Greek word and the modern English translation *believe.* The same stark differences can be seen when we look at the Greek words versus the English words *confess* and *receive.*

Confessing with Your Mouth and Believing in Your Heart

In Romans 10:9, Paul wrote, "If you confess with your mouth, 'Jesus is Lord,' and believe in your heart that God raised him from the dead, you will be saved."

Usually, well-meaning teachers and preachers convey the

meaning as follows: "If you *say* that Jesus is Lord and sincerely *agree* that God raised Him from the dead, you will be saved." But the cultural context of this statement and the Greek definition of the words translated as *confess* and *believe* represent radically different concepts and applications.

Let's take a closer look. Paul was writing to believers in Rome, explaining how they could know they were saved—and how those who didn't yet know Christ could find the way to be saved. In the first century, anyone who was a Roman citizen was required to have only one "lord," that being Caesar. So for followers of Jesus to publicly confess that Christ was their Lord was to commit treason against Caesar and the Roman government. This was a capital crime. Not only the Christian but also his or her family could be executed.

We also confuse the truth when we misinterpret the meaning of the New Testament word *believe*. In the Roman Empire, for citizens to *believe* in their *hearts* that God had raised Jesus from the dead was to be totally committed to Christ's resurrection and divinity. This was not simply mental assertion, agreeing that something was factual, just as they might agree that sunshine is warm and water is wet. This was far more than that. To believe was to commit to something in their hearts without wavering. It went to the very core of their being, the source of all decisions and behavior. To believe in one's heart was to have a whole new nature—one that was attracted to a loving, holy, and righteous God.

At the same time, to believe this in their hearts was to knowingly abandon all the rights of Roman citizenship. They would no longer have the right to work, the right to be free within the bounds of Roman law, or even the right to live. Once they owned this kind of belief in their hearts and publicly confessed Christ as

Lord, they were giving up all rights to their old way of life. They were trading a respected and highly valued citizenship in an earthly empire for a life of ridicule, rejection, and the real possibility of imprisonment or execution. Can you see the night-and-day difference between *this* application of Romans 10:9 and the modern-day application of simply agreeing to a fact?

Even the word *confess* is given a very different meaning today from what it had in the first century. The Greek word *homologeo* was coined by the conqueror Alexander the Great. The word referred to the action of a person who abandoned a rebel force to join up with Alexander's troops to fight *against* the rebels. This act reflected total agreement with Alexander's position and constituted a public demonstration of the former rebel's new allegiance. So in Paul's day, "confessing Christ as Lord" meant a publicly viewed act to abandon one's sinful past and old ways to join up with Christ to fight against one's own sin—replacing devotion to sin and self with a life-altering commitment to Christ as Lord.

This total commitment to Christ and the complete abandonment of one's personal rights can never be produced by human nature. It can take place only when a person is truly born again. And when one is truly born again, as Paul's words state, that person is saved.

Does Praying a Prayer to Receive Christ Give You Eternal Life?

The other popular formula for gaining eternal life is the teaching about receiving Christ. This modern-day concept was derived from two verses that are taken out of context. The first is John 1:12, where the apostle writes of Jesus: "But as many as received

Him, to them He gave the right to become children of God, even to those who believe in His name" (NASB). This verse is coupled with Revelation 3:20: "Behold, I stand at the door and knock. If anyone hears My voice and opens the door, I will come in to him and dine with him, and he with Me" (NKJV).

Sincere Christians, motivated by their love for Christ and their desire to see others find eternal life, tell people that they can receive Christ by opening the door of their hearts and inviting Him in. They point to John 1:12, saying this verse guarantees that people will receive eternal life if they simply receive Christ. But this approach ignores the context of both verses. Consequently, well-meaning believers may be giving people a false assurance of salvation—one that could result in their hearing Jesus say, "I never knew you; depart from me" (Matthew 7:23, NASB).

I'm sure millions of people have prayed to receive Christ and were truly born again. But praying the prayer did not save them. A person's desire to receive Christ may be the *result* of being born again, or it may be evidence of the beginning of a spiritual awakening that can lead to a new birth. However, if people have not believed in Christ in their *hearts* and totally committed their lives to following Him, then their end may be the same as if they never had any interest in Him.

To better understand how these verses have been misapplied, look at the contexts of John 1:12 and Revelation 3:20. In the first chapter of the gospel of John, the passage reads: "He came to His own, and those who were His own did not receive Him. But as many as received Him, to them He gave the right to become children of God, even to those who believe in His name, who were born not of blood, nor of the will of the flesh, nor of the will of man, but of God" (John 1:11–13, NASB). John ties all three concepts together so that they can be correctly applied only when *all three* are presented as a whole. John is saying a person becomes a child of God by receiving Christ, but he equates receiving Christ with *believing* in Jesus' name *and* being born of God, which he says is not a birth of blood (a physical birth) or a birth that is initiated by a person's will.

The context of Revelation 3:20 is even more enlightening. The popular teaching about praying to receive Christ "by opening the door of your heart" is a complete misapplication of this verse. Here is the passage in its entirety:

> I know your works, that you are neither cold nor hot. I could wish you were cold or hot. So then, because you are lukewarm, and neither cold nor hot, I will vomit you out of My mouth. Because you say, "I am rich, have become wealthy, and have need of nothing"—and do not know that you are wretched, miserable, poor, blind, and naked—I counsel you to buy from Me gold refined in the fire, that you may be rich; and white garments, that you may be clothed, that the shame of your nakedness may not be revealed; and anoint your eyes with eye salve, that you may see. As many as I love, I rebuke and chasten. Therefore be zealous and repent. Behold, I stand at the door and knock. If anyone hears My voice and opens the door, I will come in to him and dine with him, and he with Me. (Revelation 3:15–20, NKJV)

In context, Christ's invitation to open the door does not refer to a prayer of salvation but rather to an *act of repentance*—a complete about-face and change of direction. In fact, the ancient Greek word for *repent, metanoeo,* was a military command that literally meant "about face!" It was used to change the direction one was facing, as well as to change the direction soldiers were marching, by 180 degrees. In Jesus' day it was used to command a complete change of the direction of one's life—from serving self to serving God.

The invitation of Revelation 3:20 was given by Christ to a group of first-century believers who had become lukewarm in their faith. They were rich in terms of material possessions, but they were bankrupt spiritually. These people thought that because they were wealthy and had no material needs, their relationship with Christ was all well and good. But Christ's words revealed that the opposite was true. Rather than pat them on the back, He slapped them in the face. His words were both alarming and condemning. To them He said, "You are wretched, miserable, poor, blind, and naked." With symbolic expressions He advised them to pursue *spiritual* riches ("gold refined in the fire"), a cleansing of their sin and a life characterized by righteousness ("white garments"), and healing for their spiritual eyes ("eye salve") so they could begin to see the truth about His teachings and values. After all that, He told them to passionately repent, to make a total about-face from the direction they had been going to a new direction of following Him.

Only after all that did He issue an invitation to repent using a different analogy. He said, "Behold, I stand at the door and knock. If anyone hears My voice and opens the door, I will come in to him and dine with him, and he with Me." In other words, even though the lukewarm believers had offended Him, He invited them to repent. If they would do so, He promised to come into the houses of their lives and have an ongoing, intimate relationship with them. Can you see the difference between what He's saying in context and how we have so cheapened His words by turning them into a simple analogy of praying a rote prayer to receive Him?

I imagine that what I'm writing might upset a lot of people. How could so many preachers and teachers be so wrong for so many years? And even closer to home, if praying a prayer to receive Christ doesn't *cause* you to be born again, then how can you be born again and *know* it? Don't we need a definite time and place we can look back to as the moment of our conversion?

TWO QUESTIONS ON BEING BORN AGAIN

Whenever I speak on the subject of the new birth, two questions always come up. Nonbelievers ask me, "*How* can I be born again?" Professing Christians usually ask, "How can I *know* if I've really been born again?" Let me start with the first question.

How You Can Be Born Again

According to Jesus, you can no more initiate your spiritual birth than you could initiate your physical birth. You didn't decide to be born; rather your parents were physically intimate, which resulted in pregnancy and your birth. In Ephesians 2:1, the apostle Paul describes our natural state as being spiritually dead. Can dead people cause themselves to be reborn to life? Of course not! Neither can those who are spiritually dead in sin cause themselves to be born spiritually.

In Ephesians 2:4–5, Paul continues: "But God, who is rich in mercy, because of His great love with which He loved us, even when we were dead in trespasses, made us alive together with

Christ (by grace you have been saved)" (NKJV). And in Ephesians 2:8–10, the apostle goes on to say, "For by grace you have been saved through faith, and that *not* of yourselves; it is the gift of God, not of works, lest anyone should boast. For we are His workmanship, created in Christ Jesus for good works, which God prepared beforehand that we should walk in them" (NKJV).

Here is the full teaching on how to be born again. The bad news is that you can't do *anything* to initiate your spiritual birth. But the *great* news is that God offers spiritual birth and eternal life as a free gift! Sometimes that birth can be instantly seen and felt and is obvious to the spiritual newborn. Other times it takes place, and the newborn gradually wakes up to the realization that it happened. But once born, spiritual *growth* always takes place, though at different rates for different people. In the next chapter we will look at a few people in the New Testament who were born again. You will be able to see clear evidence of their new birth, even though each conversion was different.

So the answer for nonbelievers isn't what they can do to be born again. Rather, we need to tell people that God works in a person's life and that there is evidence that can help them recognize if God's Spirit is giving birth to their spirits or if He already has.

This is not as simple or straightforward as a formula. We would prefer to have more control over the process, choosing to pray a certain prayer and designating the moment when the prayer ends as the start of a person's Christian life. But Jesus and John taught something different from this. There are clear evidences or proofs of a new birth, and they do not rely on following a formula.

The evidence includes changes in a person's life such as spiritual hunger and new desires to grow and to learn more about Jesus—who He is and what He wants from us. A born-again person wants to know Christ more intimately. If these are true of a person's life, then God's Spirit is preparing the person for spiritual birth, or the new birth may have already taken place.

Still, there are people who feel it is important to connect a date and a time to their rebirth. While it is unlikely that you could pin it down with such precision, there are questions you can ask yourself. Do you believe that Jesus is the eternal Son of God who died for *your* sins and has risen from the dead? Are you willing to do whatever it takes to get to know Him more intimately? Do you really want to discover His teachings and instructions for your life? Are you willing to obey His commands as you learn what they are? Do you want to follow Him by doing whatever He tells you to do—regardless of where it may lead you or what it may cost you?

If you can answer yes to these questions, then most likely you have already been born again. These desires to know Christ—and the commitment to obey and follow Him at any cost—are not produced by our human nature. Instead, they reflect a new nature that is born of God's Spirit.

If you can't answer yes to these questions, but you *want* to be able to answer yes, I would urge you to pray and let God know exactly where you stand and what you want. Then I would urge you to begin to read the Word of God, starting in the gospel of John, and watch what happens. You will most likely fall in love with the Lord Jesus and find yourself desiring Him, His Word, and His leading in your life more than anything else. And when that happens, you will *know* that you have been born again.

How to Know If You Have Been Born Again

Believers often ask me how they can *know* if they have been born again. Again we will rely on the words of Jesus, who answered this in general terms in His talk with Nicodemus. He said, "The wind blows wherever it pleases. You hear its sound, but you cannot tell where it comes from or where it is going. So it is with everyone born of the Spirit" (John 3:8). In other words, even though you may not be able to pinpoint exactly when or how your new birth came about, if it has happened, there will be evidence (just as *hearing* the wind is evidence that there is a wind). Also, your life choices will be directed by God's Spirit rather than your own desires. You will gain a growing hunger for God's Word. You will gain a growing desire to know God more intimately. You will gain a growing desire to follow Christ by learning what He said and striving to do it. These qualities are produced and sustained only by the new nature that is birthed when you are born again.

Does this mean you will overcome your self-centeredness and will no longer be attracted to sin? Absolutely not! But it does mean that the *direction* of your will and life has changed. You have done the about-face of repentance, and your faith and trust in the Lord Jesus and His guidance will continue to grow.

Jesus also compared people who had been born again to the branches of a vine. He said, "I am the vine, you are the branches. He who abides in Me, and I in him, bears much fruit; for without Me you can do nothing" (John 15:5, NKJV). The person who is born again experiences an intimate relationship with Christ—one in which he or she is "in Christ" and Christ is in the person. The result is that the person "bears much fruit." It can be the fruit of obedience or the fruit that comes from yielding to the leading and promptings of the Holy Spirit. It can mean the "fruit of the Spirit," which Paul defines as "love, joy, peace, patience, kindness, goodness, faithfulness, gentleness and self-control" (Galatians 5:22–23). It would include the fruits of extraordinary forgiveness, mercy, and generosity. It would include a heart of gratefulness and a desire to serve others. And of course, it would include the fruit of sharing your testimony of Christ and the good news of the gospel with the people God brings across your path.

This brings up the question, what about a person who appeared to be born again—who was on fire for Christ for a number of years—and then cooled off and no longer bears fruit? Is that person born again? My answer is this: only God knows. And none of us should play God. I would direct such a person to Matthew 7:19–27 and John 15 and 1 John 2. Then I would leave the rest to the Holy Spirit.

Last but not least, the apostle John mentions one way that you can *know* beyond any shadow of doubt that you have been born again. In 1 John 2:3–6, we read, "By *this* we know that we have come to know Him, if we keep His commandments. The one who says, 'I have come to know Him,' and does not keep His commandments, is a liar, and the truth is not in him; but whoever keeps His word, in him the love of God has truly been perfected. By this we *know* that we are in Him: the one who says he abides in Him ought himself to walk in the same manner as He walked" (NASB).

A person who is wondering if he or she is truly born again can *know* that he or she has trusted Christ. The ultimate proof is that a person is keeping the commands of Christ. This would include not only Jesus' commands that are recorded in the New Testament but also promptings that a person receives from the Holy Spirit to do God's will in any given situation. John wrote, "If we claim to have fellowship with him yet walk in the darkness, we lie and do not live by the truth. But if we walk in the light, as he is in the light, we have fellowship with one another, and the blood of Jesus, his Son, purifies us from all sin" (1 John 1:6–7).

John is *not* saying that the people who have come to know Christ will be free of sin. To the contrary, he tells us that we will continue to struggle with sin during the remainder of our earthly lives (see 1 John 1:8). But while we will struggle with sin, the *direction* of our Christian lives has changed. We do an about-face, from ignoring Jesus' commands to following them more and more consistently. A person who is born again will follow Christ, embracing the truth and values of Christ and walking in the light of those truths rather than in darkness.

When I have preached on Matthew 7:21–27, people have asked me, "If these people who called Jesus 'Lord' and worked miracles weren't born again, how can I ever know if I'm truly born again? I have never worked any miracles like they did." The answer is found in Christ's declaration. He used the word *lawlessness* (NKJV) to characterize their lives. In other words, though they performed miracles through the power of faith, their lives and behavior were defined by lawlessness and sin rather than by righteousness and a lifestyle of following Jesus' teachings.

THREE REASONS YOU SHOULD BE FILLED WITH JOY AND ANTICIPATION

If you put your trust in Christ after being influenced by the teaching to invite Him into your heart, you might be concerned about your salvation. If you are now wondering whether you are a believer, here are reasons for rejoicing.

You Desire a More Intimate Relationship with Christ

This alone is evidence that you are either born again or that God is awakening your soul and calling you to Him. If you desire to know Christ more intimately, that desire comes from Him. His grace is being extended to you. You either already have a new nature that desires Him, *or* the spiritual eyes of your heart are being awakened by the Holy Spirit. If that is the case, the miracle of the new birth is at hand.

Jesus Said He Came to Call Sinners, Not the Righteous

Jesus did not come to earth to impress religious leaders. He came to hang out with people who were considered the most vile of sinners. In fact, for this He was severely criticized by the religious leaders of His day. He replied, "It is not the healthy who need a doctor, but the sick. But go and learn what this means: 'I desire mercy, not sacrifice.' For I have not come to call the righteous, but sinners" (Matthew 9:12–13). Amazing!

I am grateful that He came for those of us who were hopelessly lost. He compared Himself to a shepherd who left his flock of ninety-nine sheep to search for one that had strayed! That *one* is you...and it is I. Jesus said there is tremendous rejoicing in heaven, even among the angels that surround God, when one sinner repents (see Luke 15:7, 10). Those who are awakened to the reality that they have not yet been born again should rejoice because the awakening of their souls is likely the beginning of their new birth.

Whoever Comes to Him, He Will Never Turn Away

Here's the best news of all. Jesus invites you and me to come to Him, and when we do, He promises He won't turn us away. In

John 6:37, He said, "The one who comes to Me I will by no means cast out" (NKJV).

Do you want to follow Jesus? Do you want to discover all that He is and all that He values? Do you want to know Him intimately? As much as you want intimacy with Him, He wants it with you infinitely more. And as you will see in the following chapter, God gives spiritual birth to people who neither expect it nor deserve it—people just like you and me!

CHAPTER 7

INCREDIBLE EXAMPLES OF GOD'S BIRTHING PROCESS

*Each person's spiritual
birth is unique.*

Spend a week in the labor and delivery unit of any hospital, and you'll discover that every birth experience is unique. One of my friends was in labor for twenty-six hours, while another took less than thirty minutes. My brother-in-law's wife delivered one of her babies at a weight of eleven pounds, eight ounces. My son's first child broke the record at one of the oldest hospitals in America, with a birth length of twenty-four inches.

On the other hand, another friend's wife gave birth to the youngest baby ever to survive in America at that time. She was born at twenty-two weeks and was only a little bigger than an iPhone. Her heart was the size of the fingernail on your little finger. Among other complications, she needed open-heart surgery just to survive the first forty-eight hours. Then, to everyone's horror, a tiny ventilation tube slipped down too low and inflated, damaging her stomach. Surgeons worked for eight hours to repair the damage.

There was one miracle after another, and day after day she survived. Today, Carly Fullerton is a beautiful nineteen-year-old college freshman.

Just as every physical birth is different, so is every spiritual birth. We are not cookie-cutter beings, physically *or* spiritually. We have different spiritual births surrounded by different life circumstances. And we experience different rates of spiritual growth. Consider some of the people Jesus encountered whose spiritual birth experiences were recorded in Scripture. And contrast those experiences with others who heard the call of Christ but were *not* born again.

THE MAN BORN BLIND

For nine months a young, expectant mother and her husband looked forward to the birth of their child. At the moment of birth, there was tremendous excitement because their child was a boy! But their excitement was short lived when they discovered that their baby was blind. With that realization, their hopes and dreams were instantly abandoned.

The parents knew their son would never experience all the joys and thrills of a normal childhood and adolescence. They knew his adult years would be no happier. He would be consigned to a life of begging with no future wife and no children. They asked themselves what they had done to deserve *this*. And as if their sorrow and guilt weren't enough, they knew other people would wonder what they had done to cause this tragedy. How had they offended God to the extent that He would punish them with a blind child?

Their son grew up, and it happened that one day Jesus and His disciples passed by him. Jesus' disciples asked the same question that had plagued the man's parents: "Rabbi, who sinned, this man or his parents, that he was born blind?" (John 9:2). Jesus' answer shocked His disciples and all who listened. It also lifted a weight of guilt and sorrow that had burdened this young man, who surely had wondered what sins had brought on his blindness. "'Neither this man nor his parents sinned,' said Jesus, 'but this happened so that the work of God might be displayed in his life'" (verse 3). Unbelievable!

The apparent tragedy that had been endured by a boy and his parents was not a tragedy at all. It was a circumstance that would become an incredible tool in the hand of the same God who created the universe. Imagine the young man's thrill when he heard that his adversity *wasn't* a punishment for his or his parent's sin. He wasn't a freak accident of nature or even a terrible mistake. His life was going to serve as a demonstration of God's work. Little did he know that he would be talked about for two thousand years. (The story of his life and Jesus' words about him—and his courageous defense of the Savior—have been cherished by countless millions through the ages.)

Jesus spit on the ground and turned some dirt into mud. He spread the mud on the man's sightless eyes. Jesus then told him to wash the mud off at a nearby pool of water (see verses 6–7).

Think about this: even though the blind man was a beggar, there is nothing in the account that indicates he asked for help or that he believed Jesus could perform a miracle. Jesus took the initiative to heal him, but his healing would come *only* if the man was obedient to go to the pool and wash the mud from his eyes. The young man could have asked why he should do such a thing. He could have demanded an explanation or insisted that Jesus justify God's decision to make him blind from birth. He could even have questioned Jesus' motives and said something like, "I don't even know you! Are you nuts?" (How would *you* have responded if someone spit on the ground and tried to apply mud to *your* eyes?)

Yet the man didn't so much as question this Teacher with His twelve followers. He let Jesus apply the mud to both his eyes without objection. Then, at the Teacher's bidding, he worked his way over to the well-known pool and washed the mud off. Certainly from the time he allowed the mud to be applied until the moment he began to wash it off, he was acting in faith. Although he did not yet know who this Rabbi was, the man's heart had already been touched by the kindness of Jesus' words. God's Spirit had begun to work on his heart and mind, and though he did not yet know that Jesus was the Messiah, he took his first steps of faith in response to the Rabbi's instruction. Unbeknownst to him, God's amazing "birthing" process had begun.

Can you imagine the thrill the blind man must have felt as the clay fell from his wet eyes and he began to see? First, brilliant light replaced his world of darkness. Then color appeared, then crystal-clear images that had long been described to him but he had never seen. Oh the thrill he must have felt walking home. And because it was widely known that he was born blind, the story of his healing spread like wildfire through his community.

Jesus' miracle was so dumbfounding that at first the man's neighbors were debating if this was the same man they knew. But he insisted, "I am the man!" One by one they found their disbelief replaced with the undeniable knowledge that the man they knew to be blind could now see.

Here is where an amazing story becomes even more amazing. As his neighbors began to acknowledge that it really *was* him, they asked the next logical question—"How then were your eyes opened?" (John 9:10). "He replied, 'The man they call Jesus made some mud and put it on my eyes. He told me to go to Siloam and wash. So I went and washed, and then I could see'" (verse 11). He gave an accurate account of what had happened, but notice how he referred to Jesus. He simply said, "The *man* they call Jesus." Not the prophet, not the Messiah or the Son of God, but simply the "man."

When word of his healing made it back to the religious leaders, they had him brought to the synagogue so they could question him. After he described what had happened, the Pharisees began to debate among themselves. Some said Jesus was a sinner and had not come from God, because He had healed the man on the Sabbath. Others countered with, "How can a sinner do such miraculous signs?" (verse 16). Finally they turned to the young man and asked, "What have you to say about him? It was your eyes he opened" (verse 17). Without hesitation the man answered, "He is a prophet."

Over a short period of time, the young man's understanding of Jesus progressed from seeing Him as a mere man to seeing Him as someone much closer to God, recognizing Him as a prophet. The Pharisees were upset by this answer and dismissed the man, choosing instead to question his parents. They challenged the parents, asking if this was *really* their son. His parents said yes, this was their son. And, yes, he had been born blind. When they were asked how it was that he could now see, they simply said, "He is of age; ask him" (verse 23). The parents were afraid to take a stand for Jesus because anyone who was deemed a follower of Jesus was no longer allowed to come to the synagogue.

The religious leaders had the young man brought back before them. This time, rather than question him, they gave him *their* side of the story, hoping he would repeat it as the truth. They simply said, "Give glory to God. We know this man is a sinner." But watch what happened. The young man gave one of the most incredible defenses of Jesus recorded in the Gospels. "He replied, 'Whether he is a sinner or not, I don't know. One thing I do know. I was blind but now I see!'

"Then they asked him, 'What did he do to you? How did he open your eyes?'"

And the man began to tire of their arrogance. He said, "I have told you already and you did not listen. Why do you want to hear it again? Do you want to become his disciples, too?" (verses 24–27).

(Ouch. Way to go, former blind man!)

Bear in mind this man was talking to the most powerful religious leaders in Israel. They could banish him from the synagogue for what he had said.

The Pharisees responded by hurling insults at him and saying, "You are this fellow's disciple! We are disciples of Moses! We know that God spoke to Moses, but as for this fellow, we don't even know where he comes from."

And the young man delivered the final, fatal blow to their stand against Jesus. He replied, "Now that is remarkable! You don't know where he comes from, yet he opened my eyes. We know that God does not listen to sinners. He listens to the godly man who does his will. Nobody has ever heard of opening the eyes of a man born blind. If this man were not from God, he could do nothing" (verses 28–33).

That was more than the leaders could stand, so they angrily cut him off, saying, "You were steeped in sin at birth; how dare you lecture us!" (verse 34). Then they threw him out.

How could an uneducated beggar get the upper hand in a theological argument with the most learned men in Israel? Was he really that wise, or had his *spiritual* blindness also been healed? Had he experienced the spiritual birth that Jesus had explained to Nicodemus in John 3? I believe the answer is unquestionably yes! Look at the evidence of his spiritual birthing. First, when Jesus gave him a command, he didn't resist, but he obeyed to the letter. Second, without fear of the consequences, he defended Jesus and His actions to a powerful and hostile group of rich, educated men. But the ultimate proof that he had been born again is what happened next.

Jesus heard that the Pharisees had thrown the man out of the synagogue, and when He found him, Jesus asked, "'Do you believe in the Son of Man?'

"'Who is he, sir?' the man asked. 'Tell me so that I may believe in him.'

"Jesus said, 'You have now seen him; in fact, he is the one speaking with you.'

"Then the man said, 'Lord, I believe,' and he worshiped him" (verses 35–38).

The man fell to his knees and began to publicly worship Jesus! He could have been stoned to death on the spot—but he didn't care! His heart responded to the Savior's words with a full belief and total commitment to Jesus as God's anointed one. Without concern that he might die on the same day he had received his sight, he worshiped Jesus.

At what precise moment was this young man born again? We have no idea. The fact is, it really doesn't matter when it took place. All that matters is that he was indeed born again and his saving faith flowed freely from his heart!

A MURDEROUS THIEF AND A DYING KING

Pretend for a moment that you were present at Calvary on the day Jesus was crucified. (You are a devout Jew, and you have just returned to Jerusalem from a long journey.) As you walk through Jerusalem, you notice the commotion made by a crowd surrounding three crosses on a hill. You decide to see what is going on. Even though you don't recognize any of the men being crucified, you see a number of faces in the crowd that surprise you. You see your most revered religious leaders observing the agony of the men being executed.

If you are an evangelical Christian, it would be like seeing Billy Graham, James Dobson, Pat Robertson, and Rick Warren mingling in the crowd. You would also see your pastor and a number of local church leaders. If you are a Catholic, it would be like seeing the pope and several of his cardinals, along with priests from your local parish, mingling in the crowd.

You are stunned that respected religious leaders are focused on the man hanging on the middle cross. You hear them calling Him a fraud and a charlatan, a mouthpiece of the devil. The leaders are sneering as they hurl insults loud enough for the entire crowd to hear.

You also see city and state officials there, plus soldiers and their commanders. And there are a few of your friends from work and some of your neighbors. They too are taunting the man on the middle cross, telling Him that if He *weren't* a fraud, He would get off the cross to prove He is the Messiah. Some in the crowd are so enraged they start spitting on the man.

What would you think? Remember, you know nothing except what you have just observed. You might conclude that the guy in the middle has committed a horrible crime. No one in the crowd is paying attention to the other two criminals, but it is obvious they *really* hate the one in the middle.

Then you notice a sign at the top of the middle cross, proclaiming "King of the Jews." You would have to assume this is an impostor. Under Roman law no king can be executed on a cross. The most respectable people in Jerusalem are reviling this man, so He must be guilty of the worst crime imaginable.

Now put yourself in the place of the two men hanging on the outside crosses. If the onlookers assume that Jesus is the worst sort of lawbreaker, then the men being crucified on each side of Him will certainly come to the same conclusion. Even if you have heard rumors back in the prison cell that a man named Jesus thinks He is the Messiah, seeing Him nailed to a cross would prove He is an ordinary man. If you were a murderous thief hanging beside Jesus, the only conclusion you could draw is that He is no king and certainly not the Messiah of Israel. He *must* be a fraud.

On top of all this, you would *know* that in a few hours the impostor will be a stone-cold corpse. There is no way that He is going to get off the cross alive. You also would know that things aren't going to end any better for you. You have been convicted of the crime of murder and robbery and have been sentenced to one of the most brutal forms of capital punishment ever devised. You *know* that your fate has been sealed. You too are only a few hours from death. If ever there was a person who had *no* hope, it would be you!

Are you starting to see what the two thieves were seeing and thinking? Having already hurled insults at the man hanging between them, one thief decided to taunt Him with one more insult. He said, "If You are the Christ, save Yourself and us" (Luke 23:39, NKJV). Evidently, the man's tone of voice or the manner in which he made the statement caused the other thief to come to Jesus' defense. The second thief felt something very different rise in his heart. He condemned the first thief and defended the stranger on the middle cross.

He said, "Do you not even fear God, seeing you are under the same condemnation? And we indeed justly, for we receive the due reward of our deeds; but this Man has done nothing wrong" (verses 40–41, NKJV).

How could a thief and murderer know that Jesus, hanging on a cross just as he was, had done nothing wrong? And how could the crowd of religious leaders, government officials, and curious onlookers be so wrong about Jesus? The second thief knew that he and his counterpart were guilty of hideous crimes, and yet the crowd was ignoring both of them and focusing their anger on Jesus. What the second thief knew for sure was what the sign said above Jesus' head and what the crowd was saying. How could the thief see innocence when everyone else saw only guilt?

We will return to that question, but first consider this: violent criminals rarely take responsibility for their crimes. They have rationalizations and excuses, and they can list reasons why they aren't guilty of the crime. Even the ones who are willing to admit some responsibility still think their punishment is far *worse* than they deserve—but not this man! He not only owned up to what he had done; he truly believed that he *deserved* the torturous execution he was experiencing. Not only had he been awakened to the truth about Jesus and the truth about his own sin; his heart had been transformed into one of repentance!

He saw himself and his sin with perfect clarity. And he was beginning to see the realities of Jesus just as clearly, including the truth that He was Israel's promised Messiah. And there is only *one* explanation for this. God's grace had ripped the blinders off the thief's eyes and transformed his callous heart. God had given him a sensitive conscience, and his words gave evidence of this. His dead spirit had been brought to life—he had experienced the "second birth" that Jesus had told Nicodemus about. Without it, no one can "see" or "enter" the kingdom of God (see John 3:3–5). The criminal's spirit had been made alive, as evidenced by how he now saw himself, his sin, and his death sentence. No longer was he denying responsibility, trying to shift blame, or claiming he didn't deserve punishment. He confessed his sin rather than rationalizing it.

The second evidence of his rebirth is that he saw Jesus as He truly was—an innocent Man, wrongly condemned. But that's not all. Amazingly, the thief identified Jesus with God, as expressed by his first statement to the other thief: "Do you not even fear God?" And he didn't stop there. The ultimate evidence of his new birth was what followed—his new desire and total commitment to trust his eternal destiny to this Man even though Jesus was dying on a cross. The mob that surrounded the three crosses saw Jesus as nothing more than an impostor, but this thief saw a sinless Savior.

How could the thief look at Jesus and see a king? And not just *any* king. He saw a king who was supernatural—one who was about to leave this world through death and enter into *His* kingdom in a whole different world. Consider that the thief didn't ask for proof, as the first criminal had in his taunt. Nor did he ask to be delivered from his suffering or his approaching death. Amazingly, he looked beyond all that and said, "Lord, remember me when You come into Your kingdom" (Luke 23:42, NKJV).

This is probably the greatest demonstration of faith recorded in the Bible. All the outward evidence showed that Jesus was *not* God's Son. The crowd, including the most respected and learned religious and government officials, condemned Him as an impostor. Jesus was hanging on a cross just as the two thieves were. Jesus had received even harsher treatment from the Romans so that He was disfigured before He was nailed to the cross. All this made up the only outward evidence available to the repentant thief, but something was happening in his spirit. He chose to ignore the pitiful sight that he saw with his eyes and instead chose to *believe* what only his spirit could sense. Notice that he didn't say, "*If* you are the Christ" or "*If* you are a king." For him, there was no question. He believed in the depths of his heart that Jesus was the Christ whose life was not *ending* in death but was simply passing *through* death to enter His kingdom.

For more than three years, people kept asking Jesus to perform miracles to deliver them from illness and suffering and to provide a sign that He was truly the Messiah. But not the thief. He knew by faith that the greatest part of life was on the *other* side of the grave…a whole new kingdom with a different type of King. This was a King whose reign would never end and whose power and authority could never be deterred. Oh that *we* could see what this thief saw. Oh that our faith could be as pure and as powerful as his!

God performed a miraculous work of grace upon this thief's heart and mind. God turned a heart of stone into a tender heart of flesh. God gave him a faith that Jesus was truly a King coming into His kingdom and that Jesus could forgive his sin and cleanse him from his unrighteousness. This thief whose soul was dead in sin had been born again, spiritually birthed by God Himself. A criminal had been made alive with a brand-new desire for Jesus Christ and His righteousness.

Jesus could have said, "Do you have any idea how horrible your sin is? Do you realize what you have done and how much you are asking me to forgive?" He could have said, "You have never loved God with all your heart, and you have never loved your neighbor as yourself." He could have said, "You have paid no tithes, and you have broken all the commandments of God." Furthermore, the man had *nothing* that he could *give* the Lord—not his time, talent, or money. Nor could he make any promises of future devotion or service. He had only a short time to live. By current standards he was worthless to God's kingdom.

Jesus did not respond with silence as He had to the first thief's taunt. Amazingly, Jesus didn't even ask the second thief if he truly believed. Jesus did not question the man's sincerity or the validity of his faith. He *instantly* confirmed the thief's repentance and faith and said, "Assuredly, I say to you, *today* you will be with Me in Paradise" (Luke 23:43, NKJV). Jesus granted eternal life to this murderer who had nothing to offer but his faith.

How could Jesus so quickly pardon such an undeserving wretch? The answer is simple. The murderer had been born again, right on the cross that was ending his life. And his spiritual birth was evidenced by the fact that he did everything that Jesus requires of anyone who wishes to receive eternal life. He fulfilled the requirement of John 3:16 in that he *believed* in Jesus. He believed that He was the Christ; he believed that Jesus was sent by God.

But it didn't stop there. He believed that Jesus was going to be raised from the dead. And his faith was demonstrated by a true *repentance* from his sins and the turning of his heart away from himself toward God's only begotten Son. He did the will of the Father in that he embraced and believed in the One whom the Father had sent (see John 6:29, 40). He put all his trust in Jesus for forgiveness and eternal life.

Jesus recognized that this man had been born again. And knowing that he had been born again, Jesus could do nothing less than speak the truth—and the truth that He announced wasn't as much a pardon as it was a confirming recognition of the man's new birth. A new birth always results in eternal life. The thief would be with Jesus in paradise on that very day!

In this story the first demonstration of God's grace occurred *before* the thief said a word. God's grace was at work in the criminal's heart, mind, and vision. We know this because of the second thief's response to the words and attitude of the first thief. The first thief had access to the same evidence that was available to the second thief—the jeers of the crowd, the suffering of Jesus on the cross, the sign that called Jesus "King of the Jews." Like most of the others, the first thief was full of arrogance and sin. Like the others, this mocking thief relished the opportunity to hurl insults at the apparent impostor on the middle cross.

Not so with the second thief. Somehow his vision had been changed. Instead of seeing a fraud, he saw a Man who was a King, God's anointed One. Instead of seeing a man who was hours away from being nothing more than a corpse, he saw a dying King who was about to enter into a different kingdom—a kingdom on the other side of death. He saw a Man who not only had the power to leave earth to enter His invisible kingdom but who also had the unimaginable power to grant humans—even a criminal—entrance into His invisible kingdom. He saw Jesus not as a mere man but as the Christ who had the power to forgive him and cleanse him from the moral stain of his sins. How could a murderous thief gain such a true vision of who this Man really was? How could he gain a *desire* to repent in his final hours on earth? How could he believe that this dying Man could grant him that which no one other than God could grant?

This incredible event demonstrates what Jesus said about being born again: being birthed by God's Spirit isn't predictable (see John 3:8). It's like the wind. You don't know its beginning or where it will take you—but its evidence is undeniable. It is also a perfect demonstration of Ephesians 2:8–10. The thief's salvation had as its source the grace of God, which produced a saving faith, which produced the work of a repentant heart and a public testimony that confessed Jesus' divinity and lordship. The thief's confession of faith was simple yet complete. What a perfect demonstration of God's grace and mercy and the new birth!

OTHER GOSPEL EXAMPLES
OF THE SECOND BIRTH

There are many other wonderful examples in the New Testament of men and women who were born again. In every case we see God's undeserved grace and mercy at work prior to the event, during the event, and after the event. In every case we see undeniable evidence of a transformed life—one in which there was a complete change of direction.

Take time to examine other accounts of the new birth in the New Testament. In appendix 1 you will find the amazing story of Jesus and the woman at the well. If you want a blessing, write down the insights the Lord gives you from their stories, including the evidence of their new birth, their faith, and their repentance. These include:

1. The gentile centurion (see Matthew 8:5–13)
2. Two blind men (see Matthew 20:29–34)
3. The paralytic and his four friends (see Mark 2:3–12)
4. A blind man named Bartimaeus (see Mark 10:46–52)
5. The woman who washed Jesus' feet with her tears (see Luke 7:36–50)
6. Mary and Martha (see Luke 10:38–42)
7. Zacchaeus, a tax collector (see Luke 19:2–10)
8. The woman at the well (see John 4:7–42; see appendix 1)
9. The desperate nobleman (see John 4:46–53)

Just as there are wonderful examples throughout the New Testament of people being born again, there also are examples of those who came within reach of the Savior and God's saving grace and yet were not born again. They fell prey to the same roadblocks and deadly detours that so many people fall prey to today.

How about you? Where do you think you are in relation to God? Are you like the rich young ruler who deeply desired eternal life but could not turn away from his greater desire for the material riches the world had given him (see Matthew 19:16–23)? Or are you being spiritually awakened, seeing the Father and the Son and yourself in a whole new light? Do you sense a growing desire to follow Christ no matter what the cost? Or is He already so much a part of your life that you are embracing His Word as the basis of your decisions, actions, and faith? As much as you long to be one of His sheep, He desires to be your Shepherd infinitely more. He bids you, "Come to me, all you who are weary and burdened, and I will give you rest. Take my yoke upon you and learn from me, for I am gentle and humble in heart, and you will find rest for your souls. For my yoke is easy and my burden is light" (Matthew 11:28–30). Oh what a Savior!

PART 2

THE MISSIONS CHRIST
HAS GIVEN TO YOU

CHAPTER 8

MISSION 1: BECOME MORE INTIMATE WITH GOD

*This ranks first among your
four missions from Christ.*

M y dad was a bomber pilot during World War II. He flew forty-eight terrifying missions during his year overseas. On nearly every mission, one or more planes in his formation were shot down, and Dad watched as his friends who crewed those planes crashed and died. As he took off on each new mission, he knew that *his* plane could easily be the one that would go down next. In fact, on most of the missions he flew, his aircraft was "holed" by enemy fighters or antiaircraft fire from the ground. During one mission more than a dozen of the bombers in his formation were shot down.

Each B-24 bomber had ten crew members: four officers (pilot, copilot, navigator, and bombardier) and six enlisted men. Before each mission the officers went through a briefing in which every detail of the mission was covered. Targets were identified, the level of enemy aircraft and antiaircraft fire they were likely to encounter was detailed, and weather conditions were given. My dad listened to the mission briefings more intently than he had ever listened to anything before. He didn't want to miss even one detail, because he wanted to do everything possible to complete the mission and return to the base with his crew intact.

A single mistake could end my father's life, the lives of his men, and the lives of crew members on other planes in the formation. So learning as much as possible about the mission was crucial.

After a mission briefing, my dad would lead a separate briefing session with his men. Each crew member would hear his individual assignments. Some of the activities associated with the assignments seemed menial and insignificant, but *every one* was important to achieving the goals of the overall mission. A gunner who was distracted for even a moment could put the entire crew at risk. If the navigator made even the tiniest mistake, the aircraft could run out of fuel before making it back to its base. Every task and activity associated with accomplishing the mission was critical.

As you'll see in chapters 16 and 17, Jesus identified twenty-seven missions that the Father gave Him to accomplish on earth. After His resurrection Jesus told His disciples, "As my Father hath sent me, even so send I you" (John 20:21, KJV). The four missions He gave to His disciples apply equally to us today. He never intended His followers to become comfortable Christians who would simply go with the flow. Just as He was sent to earth to accomplish specific missions, He sends us out with specific assignments and missions.

God's will for our lives is that we pursue and accomplish four missions, along with closely related assigned activities and goals. As you learn about these missions, consider the purposes of each mission, activity, and action item. Knowing their *purposes* provides the motivation to keep at it and to overcome obstacles—and ultimately to accomplish the mission.

"How Can I *Ever* Focus on These Missions?"

When I tell people about the missions Jesus assigned to us and mention that each mission includes its own activities and specified action items, I often see a look of surprise—even dismay. The responses can be summed up like this: "Oh no, how can I *ever* focus on so many new missions and activities? I won't even be able to *remember* them, much less accomplish them."

The good news is, you don't have to memorize every detail of each mission. You only have to become familiar with them. Once you've done that, the Holy Spirit will take care of the memory work! That is one of *His* missions! Jesus said, "But the Helper, the Holy Spirit, whom the Father will send in My name, *He* will teach you all things, and *bring to your remembrance all things that I said to you*" (John 14:26, NKJV). And here's what is truly amazing. Once you prayerfully consider the missions and activities that Christ gives you, the Holy Spirit will bring them to your mind *whenever* a situation warrants it. Some will remain constantly in your focus. But others are more specific and applicable to individual situations.

Jesus did not assign missions to us to weigh us down or to make our lives unbearable. Quite the opposite. The missions are a source of light and empowerment. With an understanding of what Christ gave us to do, we can make the most of every miraculous, eternal opportunity that God brings into our paths.

I could write a book on each mission, activity, and action item that Jesus identified, but my purpose here is simply to introduce you to the four missions and give you a brief glimpse of what each one can mean to you. Christ calls all His followers to pursue four specific missions:

1. To become more intimate with God
2. To accelerate your personal growth
3. To empower other believers to follow Christ
4. To impact the lives of unbelievers in your world

MISSION 1: BECOME MORE INTIMATE WITH GOD

As we saw in chapter 3, God's number-one desire for every follower of Christ is that we experience an *intimate* relationship with Him (see Jeremiah 9:23–24; John 17:3). Everything we will become, and all that we will achieve that is of eternal worth, is dependent on God's grace and our level of intimacy with Him. And as we have seen, we love God by doing what Jesus told us to do. Obedience to Christ's commands and teachings is, literally, God's love language.

If we do not experience intimacy with God, all our efforts to achieve results of eternal worth will fall woefully short. Jesus reminded us of this in John 15:5–6 when He said, "I am the vine, you are the branches. He who abides in Me, and I in him, bears much fruit; for without Me you can do *nothing*" (NKJV). When Jesus says "nothing," He means *nothing*! Of course, we can still tell others about Christ and go through the motions of being a Christian. But if we do not live in an intimate relationship with Christ, none of our accomplishments will produce fruit of eternal value.

So the first mission Christ gave us, with its related activities and action items, focuses on our relationship with the Father and the Son.

Activity 1: Fear God

> Do not be afraid of those who kill the body but cannot kill the soul. Rather, be afraid of the One who can destroy both soul and body in hell. Are not two sparrows sold for a penny? Yet not one of them will fall to the ground apart from the will of your Father. And even the very hairs of your head are all numbered. So don't be afraid; you are worth more than many sparrows. (Matthew 10:28–31)

Jesus tells us not to fear anyone or anything, even if they can kill the body. Instead, He said, "Be afraid of the One who can destroy both soul and body in hell" (verse 28). Today the notion of fearing God is the most ignored, misrepresented, and castigated teaching of the Bible. And yet, both David and Solomon told us that the fear of the Lord is the *beginning* of wisdom (see Psalm 111:10; Proverbs 1:7; 9:10). Solomon also called the fear of the Lord "a fountain of life" (Proverbs 14:27). Fearing God adds years to your life (see Proverbs 10:27), it gives you strong confidence (see Proverbs 3:26), and it creates a place of safe refuge (see Proverbs 14:26). At the same time, fearing God teaches you to hate evil and pride (see Proverbs 8:13) and to love righteousness (Proverbs 14:2).

We have been taught, wrongly, that fearing God is the same as *revering* Him. Though the concept of reverence is included in fearing God, it does not capture the full meaning of the fear of the Lord. The words used in the Bible that are translated "fear" or "afraid" in relation to God (Hebrew, *yirah,* Greek, *phobeo*) include the reality of being terrified.

Jesus made it clear that God is *not* to be taken lightly. God so hates sin that He sacrificed His own Son by crucifixion as an atonement or covering for our sin. Do you fear cancer? How about a terrorist attack or a nuclear bomb? Do you fear an earthquake, hurricane, or tornado? Jesus said these are the *wrong* things to be afraid of, because they can kill nothing more than your body. In fact, He *commands* His followers not to be afraid of such things. But Jesus stressed that we are to fear God. The truth is that a healthy fear of a holy God is a great gift. It not only brings to us the gifts that David and Solomon revealed, but it also places God on the throne of our hearts, it positions us at a place of humility and worship before Him, and it motivates us to choose holiness over sin.

But Jesus doesn't stop there. He tells us that once we realize that God is deadly serious about sin *and* righteousness and we gain this healthy fear, then we *don't* need to be afraid! Not even one sparrow falls to the ground apart from God's perfect will, and God loves us far more than He loves a sparrow.

Our fear of God puts following Him and obeying His will at the top of our priorities. As we fear God ahead of all else, we can have the confidence that *nothing* will come upon us without first passing through His loving will for our lives. Does this mean we will be spared adversity? Not at all. Jesus said, "In this world you will have trouble. But take heart! I have overcome the world" (John 16:33). And yet, because no adversity can kill our souls or derail what God has prepared for us in eternity, we have nothing to fear.

Activity 2: Seek First His Kingdom and Righteousness

> But seek first the kingdom of God and His righteousness,
> and all these things shall be added to you. (Matthew
> 6:33, NKJV)

Our natural inclination is to pursue everything else *before* we seek God's kingdom and righteousness. Our use of time and our efforts and activities usually reflect a whole different set of priorities. But Jesus commands us to do something that runs counter to our natural inclination when He tells us to seek the things of God above all else. Why is our nature so contrary to His nature and the requirements of this second activity? The answer is simple. Christ sees this life as merely a brief precursor to eternity—it's the foreword to our book of life. On the other hand, because we exist in a time-limited realm, we view *this* life as if it were the entire book. Even though we give mental assent to the notion that this life is a momentary steppingstone into eternity, we *act* as if our day-to-day life is what counts the most. And as we saw in chapter 3, our behavior always reflects the true beliefs and priorities of our hearts.

Does this mean we should quit our jobs and pull back from all other activities to free up our time for prayer, Bible study, and missionary work? Not at all. Jesus never intended to remove us from the world. Instead He calls us to be His representatives *in* the world. But we *are* to place our relationship with God and our role as one of His subjects at the *top* of our priority list. So our pursuit of His kingdom and righteousness becomes the determining factor in our decisions and behavior.

We need to review how we allocate our time and then replace activities that have no bearing on our pursuit of God with activities that accelerate our pursuit of the things that are most important to Him. But this can't happen if we don't begin to discover, embrace, and obey the words of His Son! As we focus on the teachings of the Lord Jesus Christ, *His* values will become our values, and His priorities will become our priorities. As this takes place in our lives, the things that are of little or no importance to Him will become of little or no importance to us.

We don't have an unlimited amount of time to accomplish what Christ wants us to accomplish. James tells us that our lives are like a vapor that appears for a little while and then vanishes (see James 4:14). We usually treat time as if it were an ocean that won't run dry. Instead it's like a barrel holding a limited amount of water that will never be replenished. This is why Paul said, "See then that you walk circumspectly, not as fools but as wise, redeeming the time, because the days are evil. Therefore do not be unwise, but understand what the will of the Lord is" (Ephesians 5:15–17, NKJV). The New International Version uses these words: "Be very careful, then, how you live—not as unwise but as wise, making the most of every opportunity, because the days are evil. Therefore do not be foolish, but understand what the Lord's will is."

Going back to the second activity, to "seek first his kingdom and his righteousness" (Matthew 6:33), if we don't seek the things of God *first,* we will lose the time and opportunity to seek them at all. Because nine times out of ten, we accomplish only what is at the *top* of the list and never get around to whatever is second.

Action Item: Worship and Serve the Lord Only. There are action items associated with completing the activities that Christ gives us. These action items are specific, and they help us make the activities practical and doable. When we consider the four missions and the numerous activities that support those missions, the specified action items are the necessary steps that enable us to fulfill the assignments from Christ.

As we pursue intimacy with God and seek His kingdom and righteousness, the Lord has to be the *only* absolute Authority in our lives. When Satan tried to tempt Jesus by offering Him all the kingdoms of the world and all their glory, Jesus knew it was impossible to serve two masters. Jesus answered Satan with one of *His* mission statements that defined His earthly life. He said, "You shall worship the LORD your God, and Him only you shall serve'" (Matthew 4:10, NKJV; see Deuteronomy 6:13).

We can assume that if this was one of Jesus' earthly missions, it is a goal we need to pursue as well. Why? Because we are tempted to make money and material things our master, loving and serving them in place of God. And unlike Jesus, we *do* fall to that temptation. That's why Jesus gave us so many warnings. He said, "No one can serve two masters. Either he will hate the one and love the other, or he will be devoted to the one and despise the other. You cannot serve both God and Money" (Matthew 6:24).

Jesus was *not* saying that we should take a vow of poverty or drop out of the world of commerce or refuse to work for money. But He knew human nature causes us to crave and strive for *more* money and *more* things. So He warned us to guard against the tendency to allow money and material things to become our focus and driving purpose. And in the next specified action item, He told us *how* to do this.

Action Item: Store Up Treasures in Heaven Instead of on Earth. Jesus said, "Do not store up for yourselves treasures on earth, where moth and rust destroy, and where thieves break in and steal. But store up for yourselves treasures in heaven, where moth and rust do not destroy, and where thieves do not break in and steal. For where your treasure is, there your heart will be also" (Matthew 6:19–21).

This action item is presented in the form of a glorious command. Jesus reveals *how* we can make God our Master and limit money to the role of our servant. By *actively* setting our focus and efforts on doing things that store up treasures in heaven, we will focus less on acquiring and hoarding earthly treasures. This is critically important because our hearts (the core of who we really are) actually bond with whatever we *treasure*. God wants our hearts to bond with Him and with things of eternal purpose and worth.

The solution, as Jesus made clear, is to store up treasures in heaven. Simply stated, we do that by bearing spiritual fruit (see John 15:7–8). As we saw in chapter 6, this includes the fruit of the Spirit and the fruits of extraordinary forgiveness, mercy, and generosity. Also included are the fruit of obedience to Christ's words and the fruit from sharing your testimony of Christ and the good news of the gospel with the people God brings into your path.

According to Jesus, the only way we can bear much fruit is to abide (or dwell) in Him and let His *words* abide (or dwell) in us (see John 15:7–8, NKJV). There are no shortcuts. Christ is the Vine; we are the branches. His words are the only source of nutrition that provides the spirit and life we need to enable us to bear fruit. Until you make discovering and following His words a top priority, you will bear a modest amount of fruit or none at all. There is no other way to store up treasure in heaven apart from bearing much fruit!

Activity 3: Follow Jesus

> If anyone would come after me, he must deny himself and
> take up his cross and follow me. (Matthew 16:24)

What would happen if, instead of inviting people to pray a prayer
to receive Christ, we invited them to become *followers* of Jesus
Christ? After all, that was how Jesus called His first disciples. He
did not ask two fishermen named Peter and Andrew or a tax collector named Matthew or countless others to recite a prayer. He
invited them to follow Him. Those who accepted His invitation
did so at great personal cost. For Peter and Andrew, it meant leav-
ing behind their livelihood. For Matthew, it meant sacrificing a
lucrative tax-collection business. For another tax collector named
Zacchaeus, it meant giving half of everything he owned to the
poor and paying back, at 400 percent, the people he had cheated.

There are many others. For the woman at the well, following
Jesus meant giving up her arrogance, her self-centered ways, and
her religious biases. And for *all* who chose to follow Jesus, it meant
repentance, saving faith, and giving Jesus the place of lordship
over their hearts and lives. Unfortunately, most who heard Him,
like the rich young ruler, turned and walked away when they realized the true cost of following Him.

And yet, as compassionate as Jesus was, He never changed
His message to increase the number of people who would join up.
The path that leads to eternal life is straight and narrow. For Jesus
to represent it any other way would have been a lie of infinite mag-
nitude. He knew that *only* those who were truly born again would
follow Him, and they would do so regardless of the cost. Why?
Because when people are born again, their spiritual eyes are opened,

and they recognize that the temporary cost of following Christ is not high when compared to the riches of eternal life.

Jesus said, "For whoever wants to save his life will lose it, but whoever loses his life for me will find it. What good will it be for a man if he gains the whole world, yet forfeits his soul? Or what can a man give in exchange for his soul?" (Matthew 16:25–26). The world has nothing to offer that comes close to matching the value of our souls and the worth of eternal life.

The cost of following Him, which seems so high to a nonbeliever, is really not high at all for the person who is born again. Those who are born again *desire* to take up their cross and follow Christ—to lose their lives in loving and serving their Savior. Those who are born again, like the merchant who found a pearl of great price, know that they have found a whole *new* life in the Person of Christ. Christ and His kingdom *are* the pearls of great price, and they are worth trading everything our earthly life has to offer. After being born again, we joyfully surrender our rights to everything because we seek the joy of following Him. So the question becomes, *how* can we fulfill this third activity, that of following Christ? The how-tos are found in four specific action items.

Action Item: Hear His Words and Put Them into Practice. Jesus said, "Therefore everyone who *hears* these words of mine and *puts them into practice* is like a wise man who built his house on the rock. The rain came down, the streams rose, and the winds blew and beat against that house; yet it did not fall, because it had its foundation on the rock" (Matthew 7:24–25). As basic as this is, it is foreign to many professing Christians. Jesus made more than nineteen hundred statements that are recorded in the New Testament, but many believers are familiar with only a few of His teachings. This is a tragedy, because hearing and doing

Christ's words provide the *only* rock-solid foundation for a Christian. Everyone who is born again is a sheep in the Good Shepherd's flock. And of them, Jesus said, "My sheep hear My voice, and I know them, and they follow Me" (John 10:27, NKJV). If you are born again, you will make a practice of hearing and obeying the words of Christ.

Action Item: Do the Things That Jesus Commands. This next action item is closely related, and it is to obey all that Christ commands. As we saw in chapter 4, obeying Christ is the way to love Him in the manner *He* wants to be loved. He said, "If you love me, you will obey what I command"; "Whoever has my commands and obeys them, he is the one who loves me"; and "If anyone loves me, he will obey my teaching" (John 14:15, 21, 23). So obeying His commands is not only basic to the mission of following Jesus, but it also gives us unparalleled opportunities to love Him with the highest form of love that we can give.

Action Item: Love Jesus More Than Mother or Father, Son or Daughter. One of Jesus' statements that used to trouble me was Matthew 10:37: "Anyone who loves his father or mother more than me is not worthy of me; anyone who loves his son or daughter more than me is not worthy of me." Every time I read those words, I had to admit that I couldn't honestly say that I loved Christ more than I loved my mom or dad or my sons or daughters. Then one day the light went on. Jesus wasn't talking about our *feelings*. He was talking about loving Him the way He wants to be loved—by obeying His commands.

I love being at home with my wife and children. But there are times when I know Jesus wants me to do something else, such as preaching the gospel in another city. When I choose to follow Him even when I would prefer to stay home with my family, I am loving Him more than I love my wife or children. Discovering that I love Him by being obedient to His commands was one of the most liberating and joyful discoveries of my life.

Action Item: *Take Up Your Cross and Lose Your Life for His Sake.* In Matthew 10:38–39, Jesus said, "Anyone who does not take his cross and follow me is not worthy of me. Whoever finds his life will lose it, and whoever loses his life for my sake will find it." What looks like a burdensome, even depressing, approach to living in an intimate relationship with God is in reality a glorious opportunity. The cross is an instrument of death, and the person carrying it has no alternative but to submit to the death that awaits him. The person who is carrying the cross also has lost all his rights, including the right to live as he chooses.

So you might ask, "How could such a way of life be glorious and joy producing?" Here is how. First, when you realize you have no rights, you lose your expectations. Self-directed expectations and an entitlement mentality are the enemies of happiness. They make it impossible to be grateful, and gratefulness is the source of happiness. At the same time, when you have *no* rights or expectations, you are grateful for everything that God provides. Also, by dying to self and to your rights, you enter into a bond of intimacy with our Savior that provides joy that is not dependent on other people or circumstances. The "streams of living water" begin to flow from your innermost being, as Jesus promised in John 7:38.

Paul referred to this in Philippians 2:5–8: "Your attitude should be the same as that of Christ Jesus: Who, being in very nature God, did not consider equality with God something to be grasped, but made himself nothing, taking the very nature of a servant, being made in human likeness. And being found in appearance as a man, he humbled himself and became obedient to death—even death on a cross!"

And finally, losing our lives for Him enables us to bear fruit and make our lives count for eternity. Jesus said in John 12: "The hour has come for the Son of Man to be glorified. I tell you the truth, unless a kernel of wheat falls to the ground and dies, it remains only a single seed. But if it dies, it produces many seeds. The man who loves his life will lose it, while the man who hates his life in this world will keep it for eternal life" (verses 23–25).

Activity 4: Accept His Yoke

[Jesus said,] "Take my yoke upon you and learn from me, for I am gentle and humble in heart, and you will find rest for your souls. For my yoke is easy and my burden is light." (Matthew 11:29–30)

Though this activity may appear to be the same as following Jesus, it is actually quite different. Here, Jesus invites us to come *alongside* Him and to bind ourselves *to* Him rather than following behind. When two oxen were hitched or yoked together, one served in the dominant role and would carry the bulk of the load, while the other would balance the load. Here the Lord tells us that when we are yoked to Him, He will do the heavy work while we walk with Him. As we walk alongside Him, He will accomplish His work through us. He becomes our partner, to empower us to do that which would otherwise be impossible for us to do!

Action Item: Learn from Me. Jesus' invitation to "learn from me" should be basic in every Christian's life, and yet for most it's foreign territory. To be yoked to Christ means that He is the *first* Person we learn from—after all, He is right next to us. To keep the yoke even, we must move with Him stride for stride. Unfortunately, Jesus is usually the *last* Person we choose to learn from. We grow up learning from our parents, siblings, teachers, and peers. We learn from TV, radio, movies, and the Internet.

And yet there stands Jesus—the God who created the universe. Jesus is the only Person in history who was perfect in knowledge, wisdom, understanding, and truth. His words answer every question and resolve every problem we will face. And yet, for most professing believers, His words are the last counsel they seek rather than the first.

The good news is that it's never too late to change. Not only do we have His nineteen hundred recorded statements to learn from, but we also have the example of His life. His humility, His gentleness, His love of righteousness and hatred of deceit and hypocrisy are just a few of His traits that teach us how to live.

Activity 5: Pray That the Lord Will Send Out Laborers

> The harvest truly is plentiful, but the laborers are few.
> Therefore pray the Lord of the harvest to send out laborers
> into His harvest. (Matthew 9:37–38, NKJV)

Jesus' disciples accepted the assignment to pray for laborers. When He appeared to them after His resurrection, there were only eleven. And yet it is estimated that sixty-eight years later, when the first century came to an end, more than one *million* people were following Christ. The harvest *was* plentiful, and the Lord did answer the prayers of those who took this activity seriously.

How about you? When was the last time you prayed that the Lord would send laborers into His harvest? What kind of revival would you see in your city, state, province, or nation if you and those you influence engaged in this type of prayer every day? You can pray for laborers in general, or you can think about the various fields ready to be harvested and pray for laborers to work in those fields specifically. Take this mission seriously. Ask the Lord to send out laborers, then *watch* how He begins to answer. In these troubled times, the fields are whiter than ever. It is a perfect time for you to pursue this activity with diligence.

Activity 6: Be on High Alert for Opportunities to Serve

> Be dressed ready for service and keep your lamps burning.
> (Luke 12:35)

From time to time during World War II, my dad's bomber squadron was stationed on various islands, some of them only a mile or two wide and a couple of miles long. They had minimal land defenses against attacks from enemy aircraft. They were so concerned about a surprise attack that many nights they slept in their flight suits in case they needed to scramble the planes at a moment's notice.

Jesus gave us a similar picture in Luke 12, but He used the analogy of the servants of a groom at a wedding feast. He said, "Be dressed ready for service and keep your lamps burning, like men waiting for their master to return from a wedding banquet, so that when he comes and knocks they can immediately open the door for him. It will be good for those servants whose master finds them watching when he comes" (verses 35–37).

God is a God of purpose and accomplishment. He wants us to be the same—to recognize that we have only limited time to accomplish all He has set before us. He wants us to take Him and the four missions He has given us seriously. When Christ returns to earth, or if He calls us home prior to that time, it will be a joyous time for believers who have served Him right up to the moment He appears. It will be a tragic time for those who took His absence and mercy for granted and acted as if they would never have to give an account of how they spent their time and resources.

Let us now turn to the second mission Christ gave us, that of accelerating our personal growth.

CHAPTER 9

Mission 2: Accelerate Your Personal Growth

*When you follow Christ, you mount
up with wings, like eagles.*

Most of us see world-class athletes only when they are competing, when they are focused completely on their mission. They are fully aware of the actions necessary to succeed, so they think of nothing else but factors such as their opponents, the finish line, field conditions, and anyone or anything that stands between them and achieving their goals. And no matter the sport, how well the athletes will perform is determined by how well they prepared in the days, weeks, and months leading up to the competition.

As Christians, most of our time is spent with other people—both believers and nonbelievers. Yet our success in ministering to others is determined by our relationship with God and our efforts that further our spiritual growth. Unfortunately, this second mission from Christ—accelerating our personal growth—usually receives the least amount of our time and attention. If we want to bear much fruit and produce fruit that lasts, we need to give this second mission a much higher priority. We will never be effective in ministry and in bearing the spiritual fruit that Christ mentions unless we first concentrate on our own spiritual growth and maturity.

ACTIVITY 1: BE SET APART
AS GOD'S POSSESSION

Sanctify them by Your truth. Your word is truth. As You sent Me into the world, I also have sent them into the world. And for their sakes I sanctify Myself, that they also may be sanctified by the truth. (John 17:17–19, NKJV)

Scripture reveals six mission-specific activities and a number of closely related action items that position us for personal growth and spiritual maturity. The activities begin with being set apart, or "sanctified," for special use by God.

In Jesus' final prayer before He was arrested, He prayed for you and me. He said to His Father, "My prayer is not for them alone [His disciples]. I pray also for those who will believe in me through their message" (John 17:20). In the verses immediately preceding this, He asked His Father to sanctify His followers by God's truth (see verse 17).

The word *sanctify* is translated from a Greek root word, *hagios*, that means "to set apart for an uncommon higher use." When the term is used to describe people, it implies that a person is separated from the common values of the world to be used by God as a holy vessel. When you are born again, it is God's will for you to be set apart for righteous and holy purposes.

Jesus, having lived without sin, was able to sanctify Himself, setting Himself apart unto God. But for us to be set apart, we need to be sanctified by an outside force. That outside force is the Holy Spirit, and the means that He uses to sanctify us is truth. Sanctifying truth can be found in two places—the Word of God and the life of Christ. Jesus claimed to be the truth in human form (see John 14:6), and He told Pontius Pilate that He came into the world to "bear witness to the truth" (John 18:37, NKJV). As we meditate on God's Word and begin to embrace it by faith, the truth from His Word sanctifies us, setting us apart to be used by God and to be molded into a reflection of Christ. Jesus said to His disciples, "You are already clean because of the word which I have spoken to you" (John 15:3, NKJV). There is no other way to be sanctified than through the Word of God, both the living Word, which is Christ, and the written Word.

Action Item: Become Mature and Complete in Your Faith.

> Be perfect, therefore, as your heavenly Father is perfect.
> (Matthew 5:48)

A number of Greek and Hebrew words that appear in the Bible are translated as the English word *perfect*. Some of the words in Scripture refer to exactness or precision. Others are synonymous with what we usually mean today when we say "perfect": namely, without error or fault. But the Greek word used in Matthew 5:48 in reference to God the Father does not mean "exact" or "without error or fault." The word is *teleios,* which means "fully mature" or "complete." Jesus commands us to become mature and complete in our faith rather than remaining in a state of immaturity. When we are born again, we are born as "spiritual babies," and our natural tendencies are to continue to express the immature behavior of our previous way of life. Peter tells us to turn away from such tendencies: "Therefore, laying aside all malice, all deceit, hypocrisy, envy, and all evil speaking, as newborn babes, desire the pure milk of the word, that you may grow thereby" (1 Peter 2:1–2, NKJV).

In Matthew 5:43–48, Jesus went even further by revealing how an immature faith expresses itself: "You have heard that it was said, 'Love your neighbor and hate your enemy'" (verse 43). Next He revealed how a mature or complete faith expresses itself: "But I tell you: Love your enemies and pray for those who persecute you, that you may be sons of your Father in heaven. He causes his sun to rise on the evil and the good, and sends rain on the righteous and the unrighteous" (verses 44–45). He further explained, "If you love those who love you, what reward will you get? Are not even the tax collectors doing that? And if you greet only your brothers, what are you doing more than others? Do not even pagans do that?" (verses 46–47). When we as believers act the same way unbelievers act, our faith is immature and incomplete at best.

Then Jesus referred to His command to love our enemies and pray for those who persecute us. He implied that doing such things is the expression of a mature and complete faith: "Be perfect [mature and complete], therefore, as your heavenly Father is perfect [mature and complete]" (verse 48). With this, He commanded us to move into true maturity and completeness by acting the way our Heavenly Father acts.

Rather than hating their enemies and seeking revenge, mature believers love their enemies, blessing them and praying for them. Jesus does not command us to have loving feelings toward enemies and persecutors, but rather He instructs us to act in love. It is important to note that Jesus is instructing us in personal behavior and not in a political or national context. Also, He is not relieving us from acting responsibly toward those who inflict harm. For instance, He is not commanding a Christian wife to bless her husband by ignoring abusive behavior. He is not telling a Christian businessman to ignore unethical employees or to turn a blind eye to illegal or unethical practices. But Jesus is telling us not to let revenge or malice be the driving force of our behavior toward enemies. Even when people commit the vilest of offenses against us, we are to pray for them and personally forgive them. And in doing so, we are following Jesus' command and the first action item in becoming mature and complete in our faith.

ACTIVITY 2: PURSUE RIGHTEOUSNESS AND GODLY BEHAVIOR

Blessed are those who hunger and thirst for righteousness, for they shall be filled. (Matthew 5:6, NKJV)

Human nature is to go with the flow, simply doing what comes naturally. And, unfortunately, there is nothing natural about pursuing righteousness. Going with the flow usually plays to laziness and self-centered behavior. But Jesus gives us a mission to do the opposite—to swim upstream. In Matthew 5:6, He said those who "hunger and thirst" for righteousness will be satisfied. This may sound like a platitude, but in the ancient Greek it's far more striking. The word translated "hunger" means "famished and passionately craving." The word translated "thirst" means "thirsty to the point of pain." This implies hunger and thirst to the point of desperation. When you are that hungry or that thirsty, nothing is more important than obtaining food and water. So the question becomes, how can we gain this intensity of hunger and thirst for righteousness?

Action Item: Wake Up to Reality About Your Standing Before God.

Jesus began His Sermon on the Mount with the statement "Blessed are the poor in spirit, for theirs is the kingdom of heaven" (Matthew 5:3, NKJV). The Greek word that is translated "poor" is *ptochos,* which means "destitute," or one who has absolutely nothing! It was used to describe homeless beggars. Jesus said those who are spiritually destitute, having no spiritual worth of their own, will be the ones who are truly blessed. They are the ones who will possess the kingdom of heaven. Why? Because only the spiritually destitute realize they do not have any righteousness of their own, so they can't rely on themselves. Their only hope of entering heaven is to acquire someone else's righteousness—and that Someone is Christ! Those who see the reality of their spiritual bankruptcy run to the foot of the Cross with the heart of a beggar, desperate for mercy, forgiveness, and righteousness. They gladly exchange their sin for the forgiveness of that debt and the righteousness of Christ. In contrast, those who still believe they possess some righteousness of their own that will open the door of heaven will never run to the only One who is truly righteous. We gain a "hunger and thirst" for righteousness *only* when we see the realities of our spiritual bankruptcy.

ACTIVITY 3: "COME TO ME"

> Come to me, all you who are weary and burdened, and I
> will give you rest. (Matthew 11:28)

For those who hunger and thirst for righteousness, there is no other place to run. Jesus alone possesses the righteousness we desperately need. Paul wrote, "For He made Him who knew no sin to be sin for us, that we might become the righteousness of God in Him" (2 Corinthians 5:21, NKJV). In Christ our desperate hunger and thirst for righteousness is filled completely, and the debt of our sin is paid fully. At Calvary, Christ became our sin that we might become His righteousness before God. This incredible exchange takes place with all who are born again.

ACTIVITY 4: "LEARN FROM ME"

While the atonement satisfied the debt we owe because of our sin and applied Christ's righteousness to us, there is a practical side of our mission to accelerate personal growth. Learning from Christ is the practical way to pursue righteousness and godly behavior (see Matthew 11:29). He is our perfect example of righteous behavior, the pattern we are to model our lives after. His teachings and commands provide the perfect revelation of the righteous ways in which we are to walk. By learning from His example and abiding in His words, we discover the truth that sets us free from our enslavement to sin (see John 8:31–36), making us hungrier and thirstier for righteousness!

Action Item: Pursue Inner Righteousness Without Hypocrisy.
Jesus said to His disciples, "For I tell you that unless your righteousness surpasses that of the Pharisees and the teachers of the law, you will certainly not enter the kingdom of heaven" (Matthew 5:20). To the first-century audience, this statement would be devastating. The Pharisees and teachers of the law were known for their strict adherence to the letter of the Levitical laws. They were considered the most righteous people in Israel. Certainly Jesus' disciples thought, *How could our righteousness ever surpass theirs?*

Later on, Jesus put assumptions about human righteousness in perspective. He told the Pharisees, "Woe to you, teachers of the law and Pharisees, you hypocrites! You are like whitewashed tombs, which look beautiful on the outside but on the inside are full of dead men's bones and everything unclean. In the same way, on the outside you appear to people as righteous but on the inside you are full of hypocrisy and wickedness" (Matthew 23:27–28). The only kind of righteousness that counts is righteousness that comes from the heart—and that kind of righteousness can only come when our hearts are redeemed through Christ's atonement. When the Holy Spirit dwells within us, we experience a new level of righteousness that He expresses through us. It is the fruit of the Holy Spirit that Paul talked about in Galatians 5:22–23: "But the fruit of the Spirit is love, joy, peace, patience, kindness, goodness, faithfulness, gentleness and self-control. Against such things is no law."

Action Item: Remove from Your Life Anything That Causes You to Fall.

When I was in college, Dr. James Borror, my pastor at Scottsdale Bible Church, gave a sermon on the Lord's Prayer (see Matthew 6:9–13). When he came to verse 13, "And lead us not into temptation, but deliver us from evil" (kjv), he made a statement I'll never forget. He said he believed that we could avoid so much temptation that we needlessly go through if we would pray the Lord's Prayer every day. He wasn't talking about "rattling it off as a rote ritual," he said, but rather praying it every day, from our hearts.

In this same vein, Jesus said, "If your right eye causes you to sin, gouge it out and throw it away. It is better for you to lose one part of your body than for your whole body to be thrown into hell. And if your right hand causes you to sin, cut it off and throw it away. It is better for you to lose one part of your body than for your whole body to go into hell" (Matthew 5:29–30). Of course He was not promoting self-mutilation. He was saying that if anything in our activities or lifestyles brings a level of temptation that we can't handle, rather than continually struggling with the temptation, we should simply cut out the troublesome activity.

Most of the activities and influences that tempt us come through our visual and tactile appetites. For example, if we struggle with Internet pornography, we should install a filter and have our spouse or someone else act as the administrator. Or if we know that attending an event will put us in the path of more temptation than we can handle, we should avoid the event. By cutting off a problem at its source, we can eliminate the opportunity for temptation.

Action Item: Develop and Maintain a Grateful Spirit.

> Nevertheless do not rejoice in this, that the spirits are
> subject to you, but rather rejoice because your names are
> written in heaven. (Luke 10:20, NKJV)

Christians should be the happiest people on the planet. Why? Because gratefulness is the key to being truly happy, and Christians have more to be thankful for than any other people. However, you might be thinking that if I were familiar with your circumstances, I would understand your struggle with gratitude.

If this is your attitude, you are almost right. Most people let their circumstances determine their happiness or unhappiness. When things go great, they are happy about it, but when things go wrong, they lose their good feelings and peace of mind. But for the person who lives in an intimate relationship with God, circumstances need not determine his or her gratefulness.

In Luke 10, Jesus sent seventy men into the surrounding towns and villages, telling them to heal the sick and preach the gospel. When they returned, they excitedly reported back to Him: "Lord, even the demons are subject to us in Your name" (Luke 10:17, NKJV). Jesus told them, "I saw Satan fall like lightning from heaven. Behold, I give you the authority to trample on serpents and scorpions, and over all the power of the enemy, and nothing shall by any means hurt you" (Luke 10:18–19, NKJV). As happy as they were before He gave them this good news, they were even happier after He spoke. But then Christ announced His most important revelation on happiness. "Nevertheless do not rejoice in this, that the spirits are subject to you, but rather rejoice because your names are written in heaven" (Luke 10:20, NKJV).

Why would Jesus say that? He had just told them that He had given them tremendous authority—to walk on scorpions and snakes without being hurt, to have greater power than Satan. And yet, not even the fact that demonic spirits were subject to them should be the source of their rejoicing. Instead, only one thing should form the basis of their rejoicing—that their names were written in heaven. But why should that be the sole basis of their rejoicing?

The things that Jesus told His followers in Luke 10 apply to us today. Our rejoicing should be based on three truths:

First, the fact that we are going to heaven is evidence of the greatest miracle God has ever performed. He was able to transfer all our sin and its debt to His own dear Son. He transferred all of Christ's righteousness to us. He made people who were dead in sin alive in Christ. He demonstrated His loving-kindness, righteousness, and justice in the single greatest act of mercy in history.

Second, when we were dead in our sins, having absolutely no hope of gaining eternal life, we were born again by God's ultimate act of grace. Because of God's action, we were forgiven of our sins and redeemed by the shed blood of God's Son. We gained a heart to repent and believe. Oh what a Savior! Oh what grace! Knowing this, how could we ever be unhappy or fail to be grateful?

Finally, while everything else we possess can be lost or taken away, eternal life cannot be taken away. It cannot be weakened or limited by anything on earth.

Does this mean we can't be sad or grieve? Not at all. Whenever we lose anyone or anything that is dear to us, of course we will be sad and grieve. Jesus wept at the thought of Lazarus's death even though He was only minutes away from raising him from the dead. But even when we experience sadness or grief, we can still rejoice in the fact that we have eternal life. Rejoicing is not a feeling; it's an action inspired by faith. It's the way we express thanks to God for His love, mercy, forgiveness, and salvation. When the source of your rejoicing is the fact that you have eternal life, you can go through anything! Jesus said to His disciples, "Blessed are you when people insult you, persecute you and falsely say all kinds of evil against you because of me. Rejoice and be glad, because great is your reward in heaven, for in the same way they persecuted the prophets who were before you" (Matthew 5:11–12). Even when we are abused by others, we can rejoice, because we know our reward is in heaven and cannot be taken away.

Action Item: Don't Give In to Fear.

> Why are you so afraid? Do you still have no faith?
> (Mark 4:40)

We live in a culture permeated with anxiety and fear. Failing economies, terrorism, violent crime, widespread joblessness, and the rising cost of living are just a few of the circumstances that can make even the most stout of heart fearful. It can seem as if we are floating on a small raft in the middle of rough seas with little more than a broken oar to help us get back to shore. And yet, Jesus commands us to "fear not." He tells His disciples, "In this world you will have trouble. But take heart! I have overcome the world" (John 16:33).

It is one thing to know that Jesus tells us not to fear. But how can we be delivered from the fears and anxieties we struggle with? The answers are found in six steps that the Savior asks His followers to take:

Step 1: Take charge of your heart. The first task in overcoming fear is to take charge of your heart. Remember, your heart is not just your emotions; it is the core of who you are.

Human nature is to let our hearts be controlled by outside forces. We talk about "falling in love," as if we have no control over the process. We get angry and blame someone else for causing our anger. We experience adversity and let the adversity take charge of our hearts. We feel uncertain or fearful and choose to let fear take charge of our hearts.

This is the opposite of what Jesus teaches. In John 14:1, 27, Jesus told His disciples, "Do not let not your hearts be troubled." He was telling them, "Wrestle your heart away from the circumstances and fear that control it. Don't simply go with the flow."

But once you've taken charge of your heart, how can you guard it and prevent it from falling back under the control of fear or any other circumstance? Jesus answers with the next step.

Step 2: Trust in the Father and the Son. It's easy for us to feel self-sufficient. We are responsible adults, and we like to think we have things under control. But we are not capable of protecting our hearts. Adverse circumstances and fear are like schoolyard bullies, and we are like ninety-pound weaklings. Our only hope is to quickly turn our hearts and their protection over to Someone a lot stronger and more powerful than life's bullies.

Jesus gave us the secret to guarding our hearts when He said, "Trust in God; trust also in me" (John 14:1). When you pass your heart over to the Father and the Son, you win, and the bullies are left powerless. Referring to His sheep, Jesus said, "My sheep listen to my voice; I know them, and they follow me. I give them eternal life, and they shall never perish; no one can snatch them out of my hand. My Father, who has given them to me, is greater than all;

no one can snatch them out of my Father's hand" (John 10:27–29). Our security and trust start with hearing His voice and following Him. Jesus has given us more than one hundred promises and more than one hundred forty commands. We put our trust in Him when we hear His word and by faith step out and *do* what He says. Trusting Him is not a feeling; it's an action in response to His word or His prompting.

Step 3: Be courageous. After Jesus fed five thousand men and the women and children who were with them, He told His disciples to get into their boat and cross the lake. Then He dismissed the crowd and climbed a hill to get alone to pray. About three o'clock in the morning, the boat was far from shore and making slow progress due to high winds and rough seas. Suddenly the disciples saw an image approaching them on the water. They screamed in terror, thinking it was a ghost. Then they heard Jesus say, "Take courage! It is I. Don't be afraid" (Matthew 14:27). Upon hearing His words, their fears were instantly relieved.

How do we explain their sudden change? The words from the Savior vaporized their fears. A simple statement sandwiched between two commands changed their hearts. The commands were "Take courage" and "Don't be afraid." But the statement in the middle was what empowered the disciples to obey both commands. A simple yet infinitely powerful revelation: "It is I." The only reason for them to be courageous was because Jesus had come to them. Where they once saw what they thought was a ghost, they now saw the Savior.

No matter what we go through, as soon as we receive a word from Jesus, we realize that our world is not out of control. Jesus is close at hand, and peace will replace our fears. Peter was so emboldened by the presence of the Lord that he said, "Tell me to come to you on the water" (verse 28). Jesus replied with a single word: "Come" (verse 29). Jesus' word was so powerful it not only created faith in Peter, but it also empowered him to do the miraculous—walk on water. But then Peter saw the wind and quickly forgot Jesus and His word. He was distracted by circumstances, and fear vaporized his faith.

As he began to sink, he cried out, "Lord, save me!" (verse 30). Jesus grabbed him and said, "You of little faith, why did you doubt?" (verse 31). As they got onto the boat, the wind instantly died down. The purpose for the storm had passed, and the lessons had been learned. Adversity tests and refines our faith. The source of courage and faith is the words of Christ that assure our hearts that He is present. And because Christ reminds us that He is with us, we have no reason to fear.

Step 4: Stop doubting and start believing. On the day of Jesus' resurrection, some of the disciples were hiding in fear behind locked doors. Without opening the door, Jesus appeared in their midst. However, Thomas was not there, and when the other disciples told him later that they had seen the Lord, he was openly skeptical. "Unless I see the nail marks in his hands and put my finger where the nails were, and put my hand into his side, I will not believe it" (John 20:25).

A week later they were again together in the house, but this time Thomas was with them. The apostle John recorded what happened next. "Though the doors were locked, Jesus came and stood among them and said, 'Peace be with you!' Then he said to Thomas, 'Put your finger here; see my hands. Reach out your hand and put it into my side. Stop doubting and believe.' Thomas said to him, 'My Lord and my God!' Then Jesus told him, 'Because you have seen me, you have believed; blessed are those who have not seen and yet have believed'" (John 20:26–29).

Jesus told Thomas (and you and me) to "stop doubting and believe." And Christ provided a detail just for us, for those who have not physically seen the Lord: when we replace doubt with belief, He will bless us in an added way. He will show us a way to love God and bless Him with a level of faith that would not be possible if we, like Thomas, had seen Him. Regardless of how such blessings are manifested and experienced, He has promised them to us if we will take the step to stop doubting and start believing, acting upon His words.

Step 5: Don't worry about your life, food, shelter, or other physical needs. If ever there was a command and a promise from the Lord that we ignore, it's this one! In Matthew 6:25, Jesus tells us, "Do not worry about your life, what you will eat or drink; or about your body, what you will wear." He began the full verse with the word "therefore," which means that what He said previously (in verse 24) is the foundation of our ability to stop worrying. Simply stated, Jesus assured us that we can't serve two masters—money and God. We have to choose between them.

Once you choose to make God your Master, you can stop worrying about material needs. Jesus does not deny the legitimacy of these needs. He simply says they are not to be a significant focus of your devotion, energy, or pursuit. And above all, they should never be a cause of worry or fear. If these things do give rise to stress or anxiety, then you have reason to question whether God is truly your Master. You may well be serving a different master, giving money or material possessions control of your heart. You cannot serve both, only one!

Here are the reasons why we don't need to worry about food, shelter, or clothing. Jesus said, "Is not life more important than food, and the body more important than clothes? Look at the birds of the air; they do not sow or reap or store away in barns, and yet your heavenly Father feeds them. Are you not much more valuable than they? Who of you by worrying can add a single hour to his life?" (Matthew 6:25–27). When we make God our Master, we stop worrying about money and material possessions—even the necessities of life. Our Heavenly Father loves us so much He will provide all our needs.

Step 6: Don't fear those who can kill only the body. As we saw in chapter 8, our first activity in the pursuit of intimacy with God is to fear Him alone. In Matthew 10:28, the disciples were told whom not to fear—namely those who can kill the body but not the soul. Jesus knew His disciples would face tremendous persecution, yet they were not to fear any person. Today most of us don't worry about being murdered. But how about other things that kill the body we inhabit? Every year millions of people are diagnosed with potentially deadly diseases. After my son's cancer diagnosis, the words of Matthew 10:28 jumped off the page at me. God confirmed in my heart that the worst outcome of my son's cancer would be to kill his body. But that was not to be feared, because his soul was secure for eternity.

Jesus does not tell us to eliminate our *emotions* of fear but rather not to *behave* in fear. We can't control our emotions, but we can control our choices and our behavior. When we embrace the fact that our earthly lives are temporary, while our lives in Christ are eternal, our behavior starts to reflect that truth. The amazing thing is that as we live in faith that our lives are in His hands, our emotions will follow our behavior. The fears that once were debilitating are soon little more than momentary distractions. But it all starts with our faith in Him and acting on His commands and promises.

ACTIVITY 5: LIVE IN THE PRESENT MOMENT

One of the greatest obstacles to following the promptings of the Holy Spirit and living a life of faith is that our minds and hearts tend to focus on the future or the past. The future could be ten minutes from now; and the past is not just our childhood or last year but also what happened five minutes ago. If we let our focus remain on any of these, we are not living in the moment. For example, if a colleague offends you at work, and you are still being affected by it when you arrive home that evening, you are not living in the moment. Or if you come home at six o'clock and are distracted by concerns related to a meeting coming up the next morning, you are living in the future and won't be attentive to your family.

In Matthew 6:34, Jesus commands, "Therefore do not worry about tomorrow, for tomorrow will worry about itself. Each day has enough trouble of its own." And once again He begins this statement with "therefore." So the basis for not worrying about tomorrow is the statement that immediately precedes this. Jesus said in verses 32–33, "Your heavenly Father knows that you need them [food, clothing]. But seek first his kingdom and his righteousness, and all these things will be given to you as well." The reason we don't have to worry or fear tomorrow or a thousand tomorrows is because God will give us all our true needs when we pursue His kingdom and righteousness.

But living in the future isn't the only distraction from pursuing God. We can be distracted by the past as well. It's easy to be mired in regret over past mistakes, or in anger and hurt over an offense that was inflicted by someone else. My dad would become so distressed about missed opportunities and past hurts that he often was consumed by bitterness, even to the point of excessive drinking. I've known people who have wasted years by focusing on the past. Jesus said, "No one who puts his hand to the plow and looks back is fit for service in the kingdom of God" (Luke 9:62).

If we are not to live in the future and we are not to look back, where does that put us? It puts us right where God wants us—in the moment! Only when we live in the moment can we be His true representatives to everyone He brings into our paths.

ACTIVITY 6: OVERCOME TO THE END

Shortly before His arrest, Jesus told His disciples, "In this world you will have trouble. But take heart! I have overcome the world" (John 16:33). Jesus never promised His followers an easy life. In fact, His call was "If anyone would come after me, he must deny himself and take up his cross and follow me" (Matthew 16:24). There is nothing easy about dying to your own rights, needs, and desires. He told His disciples that they would be scattered, persecuted, and hated. But at the same time, He told them not to worry, for He has overcome the world. And later, in His revelation to the apostle John, He gave the command to all His followers to overcome. In fact, this is such an important mission that He gave twelve promises to those who would overcome. Here are the promises:

1. They will receive the right to eat from the tree of life in paradise (see Revelation 2:7).

2. They will not be hurt by the second death (see Revelation 2:11).

3. Jesus will give them "hidden manna," supernatural nourishment (see Revelation 2:17).

4. He will give them "a white stone with a new name written on it" (see Revelation 2:17).

5. Jesus will give that person "authority over the nations" (see Revelation 2:26).

6. They will be clothed in white (see Revelation 3:5).

7. Their names will never be erased from the book of life (see Revelation 3:5).

8. Jesus will acknowledge their names before the Father and His angels (see Revelation 3:5).

9. They will become pillars in the temple of God and will never have to leave it (see Revelation 3:12).

10. Jesus will write the name of God and the city of God upon them (see Revelation 3:12).

11. Jesus will write upon them His new name (see Revelation 3:12).

12. They will sit with Jesus on His throne (see Revelation 3:21).

This raises the obvious question, what does Jesus mean when He tells us to overcome? He tells us in Revelation 2:26: "To him who overcomes *and does my will to the end,* I will give authority over the nations." In Revelation chapters 2 and 3, Jesus gave specific messages to His followers in seven different cities. His message to the believers in each city ended with the assignment to overcome.

Overcoming doesn't mean surviving or existing. It doesn't mean just getting by or marking time. As seen in Jesus' statement in Revelation 2:26, it means being fully engaged in the mission of *doing God's will* right up to your final breath.

The twelve promises Christ made to those who overcome are far-reaching. Some will not become clear to us until we are face to face with Him. But one thing is certain: overcoming is critical. In this world there are three keys to overcoming or doing His will to the end. First, we must continually discover what Jesus said (His words, commands, and promises) and then obey what He said. Second, we must become committed and accountable to others in the body of Christ who also are committed to discovering and doing His will. And, finally, we must rely fully on the ministries of the Holy Spirit to continually lead us in our walk with Christ.

As we think about overcoming to the end, we come to the third of the four missions that Christ gave us. This one moves from personal growth and spiritual maturity to reaching *outward* to others, beginning with fellow believers.

CHAPTER 10

MISSION 3: EMPOWER OTHER BELIEVERS TO BETTER FOLLOW CHRIST

"Lovest thou me more than these?"

As Christians, we recognize the importance of evangelism. Jesus commissioned His disciples to go throughout the world and preach the good news of God's gift of eternal life through the sacrifice of His Son. Twenty centuries later, we should be no less dedicated to proclaiming the gospel. And yet, as important as it is to reach the unbelieving world, Jesus gave us another mission that is just as important. Jesus asked Peter three times, "Do you love me?" (see John 21:15–17). Each time, when Peter answered yes, Jesus responded with commands that defined Peter's missions to minister to believers.

Specifically, Jesus told Peter to feed, nurture, lead, and take care of His sheep and lambs. Oh how the Good Shepherd loves

His sheep! And if this is how Peter was to demonstrate his love of the Savior, it also is a way we can express our love for Him. To this end, Jesus gave His followers five activities that will help us fulfill this mission of empowering believers to better follow Christ.

ACTIVITY 1: FEED AND SHEPHERD HIS SHEEP

The writer to the Hebrews wrote, "Without faith it is impossible to please God" (11:6). Paul wrote that "faith comes by hearing, and hearing by the word of God" (Romans 10:17, NKJV). In Romans 10:14, he asked, "How shall they hear without a preacher?" (NKJV). In the Greek the word translated as "preacher" is a present tense verb. It could more accurately be rendered "one proclaiming." So the verse literally reads, "How shall they hear without someone proclaiming to them?" The first mission of any believer in relation to other believers is to help them grow their faith by proclaiming the Word of God to them. That is how we feed Christ's sheep.

Yet feeding the sheep is only one of the mission activities. The other is to shepherd, or take care of, His sheep. We do that by leading other Christians by our example. Sheep follow shepherds. We must walk the path that we want them to follow. The word that is used in John 21:15–17 for "shepherding" includes the idea of tenderness. We are to tenderly take care of the believers we are shepherding. We guide them with love and encouragement. Sheep are easily scared and scattered. Their lives and futures depend on the nurture, care, and protection of a shepherd. Is this how you deal with your spouse, your children, and other believers you relate to? The Great Shepherd wants you to do for His sheep what He has done and is doing for you.

Action Item: Love One Another As He Has Loved Us.

In John 13:34, Jesus revealed an action that is central to shepherding His sheep. He said, "A new command I give you: Love one another. As I have loved you, so you must love one another." He repeated this command minutes later when He said, "My command is this: Love each other as I have loved you. Greater love has no one than this, that he lay down his life for his friends. You are my friends if you do what I command" (John 15:12–14). The action that guides us in shepherding other believers is to love them the way Christ has loved us. The two questions now become, how has He loved us, and how can we follow His example in loving the believers He brings into our lives?

Christ loves us in so many ways. He is light in our darkness, showing us by His words and the example of His life the way we should go. He lived His life in righteousness for us, and He died for us. He tells us eternal truths, instructing us when His truth is contrary to our values, priorities, and lifestyles. He shows us tremendous patience, grace, and mercy. He is our best Friend and serves us in ways that we can't even imagine. And though we are not capable of loving one another to the *degree* that He loves us, we can love one another in the same *manner* as He loves us.

Action Item: Become Unified in Christ.

In His final prayer before His arrest, Jesus told His Father:

> My prayer is not for them [His disciples] alone. I pray also
> for those who will believe in me through their message
> [i.e., you and me], that all of them may be one, Father, just
> as you are in me and I am in you. May they also be in us

> so that the world may believe that you have sent me. I have
> given them the glory that you gave me, that they may be
> one as we are one: I in them and you in me. May they be
> brought to complete unity to let the world know that you
> sent me and have loved them even as you have loved me.
> (John 17:20–23)

How important is it to the Lord that we be unified with other believers? It's so important that as His crucifixion drew near and He had one last moment of intimate prayer with the Father, He emphasized His desire that we be unified—*three* times! Is unity with other Christians a desire of your heart? Knowing that Jesus greatly desired it, shouldn't it become a major priority for each of us? Are you willing to make Jesus' great desire a high-priority action in your life?

But how can we be unified when we have so many doctrinal differences? It is possible, but we never will be unified around doctrine. The basis of our unity can be only one thing—the desire to discover and do what Jesus commanded and taught. He said, "If anyone would come after me, he must deny himself and take up his cross and follow me" (Matthew 16:24). That verse contains the secret to unity with other Christians. If the focus of your life is to deny yourself, take up your cross, and follow Jesus, then you can have unity with *any* other believer who wants those same things. The more closely we follow Christ, the closer we will grow in unity with others who follow Him.

The problem is that most American Christians make their Christianity about everything *but* following Christ. I'm not saying doctrine is unimportant. Sound doctrine is extremely important.

But it was never meant to be our primary focus. Denying self, taking up our crosses, and following Christ were always meant to be our chief focus.

The diagram below depicts a tendency for churches and their members to focus on their doctrinal distinctives. They concentrate on their unique approaches to evangelism, prophesy, worship, the gifts of the Holy Spirit, and so forth. In other words, they focus on the things that make them different from other Christians, which creates walls of separation between them and other churches.

GOD

Words and Teachings of Jesus

○ Churches and their members

↗ Focus on distinctives

| Walls created by denominational traditions and doctrinal distinctives

The next diagram shows what would happen if churches and individual believers would make discovering and doing what Jesus said the focus of their ministry and lives. The walls that previously separated believers would not disappear, but they would no longer divide the body of Christ or prevent unity.

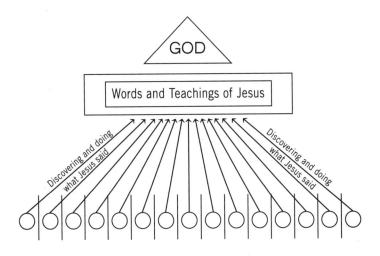

As we dedicate ourselves to following Jesus by discovering and doing what He instructs and commands, we move closer to Him. And the closer we move toward Christ, the closer we move toward unity with one another.

To this end, a growing number of Christians, churches, and organizations (such as Extraordinary Women and the American Association of Christian Counselors) are working to encourage churches and individual believers to focus on discovering the teachings of Christ and applying them to every area of life.

ACTIVITY 2: STRENGTHEN YOUR BROTHERS AND SISTERS

At the Last Supper, Jesus told Peter that Satan would sift him like wheat. In other words, Peter was going to face a terrible trial. But Jesus also told him, "I have prayed for you, Simon, that your faith may not fail" (Luke 22:32). Then He gave Peter a mission activity that he was to focus on once he repented and reengaged in the faith. He said, "And when you have turned back, strengthen your brothers." And knowing the Good Shepherd's love of His sheep, we can safely assume that He would have us engage in this mission activity with the same commitment He was demanding of Peter.

So the question is, how can we strengthen other believers? Here again, Jesus doesn't leave us ignorant. He tells us to love one another in the same manner that He has loved us. He loves us by giving us His Word to guide us through each day; by listening to our hearts—our joys and our sorrows; by extending to us an ear when we need to be heard; by giving us comfort when we need to be comforted; by giving us encouragement when we need to be encouraged; by nurturing us in our relationship with Him; and by giving us the Holy Spirit to empower us to hear and follow His words. We can do all these with one another. And we can do it all with love, patience, and tenderness, just as He does with us. And last but not least, we can pray for one another.

ACTIVITY 3: TEACH OTHERS TO OBSERVE EVERYTHING CHRIST COMMANDED

For a number of years, I was involved with an evangelical organization in which adherents frequently quoted the Great Commission—but only part of it. We quoted Matthew 28:19: "Go ye therefore, and teach all nations, baptizing them in the name of the Father, and of the Son, and of the Holy Ghost" (KJV). But we overlooked Jesus' focal point and what He emphasized in this statement, which is contained in verse 20: "and teaching them to obey everything I have commanded you."

To skip verse 20 is to end the statement midsentence. Doing so is not only a grammatical error, but it omits the single most important part of the Great Commission. Remember, Jesus didn't speak in verses; He spoke in sentences and phrases. If you read Matthew 28 without the verse numbers, when you got near the end of the chapter, it would say, "Therefore go and make disciples of all nations, baptizing them in the name of the Father and of the Son and of the Holy Spirit, and teaching them to obey everything I have commanded you." Christ told us to make disciples by teaching believers to obey His commands and teachings.

It is impossible to overstate the importance of Jesus' teachings and commands. Obeying what He said is not only the way we express our love for Him (see John 14:15, 21, 23); it also is the way we become His disciples. Further, it is the way we lead other believers into discipleship! Obedience to Christ is central to our relationship with Him. Those who "hear the word of God and keep it" are blessed (Luke 11:28, NKJV). And Jesus said that if you *do* the will of the Father, you will be a member of His family (see Matthew 12:50)!

And now we come to the last of the four missions that Christ has given us. This one calls us to impact the lives of nonbelievers for the kingdom of God.

CHAPTER 11

MISSION 4: IMPACT THE LIVES OF NONBELIEVERS

"Look at the fields, for they are already white for harvest!"

Can you remember who introduced you to the reality and truth of the Person of Jesus Christ? Think back to that time. What was your initial response? How long did it take from the time you first heard about Christ until you made a full commitment to follow Him?

How many other people had a positive effect on your attitude toward Christ prior to your making a total commitment? What would your life be like today had they never reached out to you? For the Christians who spoke to you about Christ, you were a white field ready for harvest, and you were someone whom God brought across their path.

Reaching out to nonbelievers and sharing the good news of the reality of Jesus Christ is not just an option for Christians; it is a mission that Jesus commands us to undertake. In fact, He gave us nine mission activities that focus on our reaching out to the nonbelievers that He brings to our attention. The first activity relates to timing. It is our nature to procrastinate, but there is no time for that when it comes to sharing the gospel.

ACTIVITY 1: REACH OUT *NOW*

It is easy to miss the opportunity of the moment because we are thinking about the near past or the near future. At work we may walk past the receptionist without saying a word because we're thinking about a meeting that's coming up in twenty minutes or an argument we had with our spouse the night before. Our natural inclination is to let our focus remain on ourselves and our circumstances. In John 4:35, Jesus said, "Do you not say, 'There are still four months and then comes the harvest'? Behold, I say to you, lift up your eyes and look at the fields, for they are already white for harvest!" (NKJV).

Jesus tells us to stop procrastinating, to open our eyes and look at the fields right in front of us. They are already white for harvest. We are commanded to come into the moment, see the opportunities, and act on them without delay. When I walk into work, every person God brings into my path will be my white field at that moment. We are to be Jesus' representatives to whomever He puts before us.

When I get on an airplane tomorrow, my white field will be the flight attendants, the passenger in the seat next to me, and others. Does this mean I preach to everyone in my path? Not at all. But it does mean that if someone needs to talk, I become the compassionate ears of Christ. If someone needs a hug, I become the arms of Christ. If someone needs encouragement, I become Christ's giver of hope and encouragement. And if someone needs to hear the gospel, I become the preacher of His gospel.

Jesus not only commanded this of us; He demonstrated it every day of His earthly life. He gave us this mission activity immediately following His encounter with the woman at the well. As it turned out, an entire village was evangelized because Jesus came into the moment and focused on a woman who was His white field waiting for harvest. How many white fields will you encounter in the next twenty-four hours? in the next week? in the next year? Will you be caught looking down, or will you look up and reap the harvest? Undertaking this activity has the power to turn every day into a tremendous series of blessings for you and for those you encounter.

ACTIVITY 2: OPEN YOUR EYES TO THE WHITE FIELDS

Every morning when you wake up, tell the Lord you understand that today you are on a mission for Him. Then ask Him to open your eyes to every white field around you that day. Ask the Holy Spirit to make you sensitive to His promptings. Realize that you have the power to express the love of Christ in different ways, whether it's giving someone a smile and a greeting, or encouraging someone with a word, or applying God's Word to a situation someone is going through.

Activity 3: Get Involved in Sowing and Reaping

Sowing and reaping are crucial in accomplishing the mission of impacting the lives of nonbelievers. After Jesus told His disciples to lift up their eyes and look at the fields, He said, "And he who reaps receives wages, and gathers fruit for eternal life, that both he who sows and he who reaps may rejoice together. For in this the saying is true: 'One sows and another reaps.' I sent you to reap that for which you have not labored; others have labored, and you have entered into their labors" (John 4:36–38, NKJV).

We sow the gospel by spreading God's Word like seeds in the minds of others. We can share by relating specific statements from the Word of God to virtually any situation a nonbeliever is going through. You might share Matthew 11:28–30 with a person in the midst of adversity or deep sorrow. Jesus said, "Come to me, all you who are weary and burdened, and I will give you rest. Take my yoke upon you and learn from me, for I am gentle and humble in heart, and you will find rest for your souls. For my yoke is easy and my burden is light."

I often incorporate God's Word into conversations and even business seminars that I teach, in a nonthreatening way. I have taught executives of Fortune 500 companies a seminar about achieving extraordinary outcomes. Two of the strategies I teach are those of effective partnering and a process called "vision mapping." When I talk about partnering, I quote Proverbs 15:22, "Plans fail for lack of counsel, but with many advisers they succeed," and Proverbs 11:14, "Where there is no counsel, the people fall; but in the multitude of counselors there is safety" (NKJV).

When I talk about vision mapping, I quote Proverbs 29:18: "Where there is no vision, the people perish" (KJV). Sowing seeds can be as simple as that. In my experience, those seeds often take root and result in conversations that lead to sharing my faith in Christ. And just as often, they are sown without an immediate indication of the listeners' interest. In those instances, I trust God to nurture those seeds.

On the reaping side, remember that it is never your job to try to *persuade* a person to commit his or her life to Christ. You simply share what the Holy Spirit prompts you to say or do, whether it be your testimony, the Word of God, or the godly solution to a problem. It is the Holy Spirit's responsibility to draw them into God's kingdom, not yours. And yet, as you avail yourself of His leading, He will give you the joy of reaping where others have sown.

ACTIVITY 4: BEAR FRUIT

In His conversation with His disciples at the Last Supper, Jesus revealed one of the most important activities the disciples were to undertake (see John 15:1–8). And because of the black-and-white nature of His statements about this activity, we must see it as an assignment He gives to all His followers.

Jesus compared His disciples (and us) to the branches of a grapevine and compared Himself to the trunk of the vine. He compared God the Father to the Gardener who cares for the vine. Later, Christ revealed that His words are the life-giving sap that keeps the branches healthy and enables them to bear fruit. In this analogy, He revealed seven truths that must have been startling to His disciples:

1. The purpose of the vine and its branches is to bear much fruit (see verse 2).

2. Healthy branches (followers of Christ) bear a lot of fruit (see verse 5).

3. All the life-giving, fruit-producing sap in the branches comes from the vine (Christ) (see verses 4–6).

4. If the branch doesn't remain in a healthy relationship with the vine, it can't bear fruit (see verses 5–6).

5. If the branch does remain in a healthy relationship with the vine, it *will* bear much fruit (see verse 5).

6. If the branch does not bear fruit, then it is cut off and thrown away (see verse 6).

7. If the branch bears fruit, it is pruned so it can bear even more (see verse 2).

Jesus reveals two additional truths in this passage that contain incredible promises. First, His *Word* makes us clean. Second, if *we* abide (dwell or remain) in Him and His words abide (dwell or remain) in *us*, then we can ask whatever we wish, and it will be given to us—and we will bear much fruit. Amazing! He promises that when we meditate on His words and do them, His words will make us clean. Further, His words will become the master key to receiving what we pray for and to our bearing much fruit. If you think this sounds too good to be true, read the full passage:

I am the true vine, and my Father is the gardener. He cuts off every branch in me that bears no fruit, while every branch that does bear fruit he prunes so that it will be even more fruitful. You are already clean because of the word I have spoken to you. Remain in me, and I will remain in you. No branch can bear fruit by itself; it must remain in the vine. Neither can you bear fruit unless you remain in me.

I am the vine; you are the branches. If a man remains in me and I in him, he will bear much fruit; apart from me you can do nothing. If anyone does not remain in me, he is like a branch that is thrown away and withers; such branches are picked up, thrown into the fire and burned. If you remain in me and my words remain in you, ask whatever you wish, and it will be given you. This is to my Father's glory, that you bear much fruit, showing yourselves to be my disciples. (John 15:1–8)

ACTIVITY 5: BE HIS WITNESS

Jesus' last statement to the apostles (and to all His followers) before He ascended into heaven is recorded in Acts 1:8: "But you will receive power when the Holy Spirit comes on you; and you will be my witnesses in Jerusalem, and in all Judea and Samaria, and to the ends of the earth." The activity is to serve as witnesses who publicly and privately testify about Jesus, His work, and His words. The two initial actions for the apostles related to this activity were (1) to wait until the Holy Spirit came upon them and infused them with power and then (2) to be His witnesses, starting in Jerusalem, then to all Judea, then to Samaria, and ultimately to the entire world.

What do these actions mean for us? First, we must realize that it is the Holy Spirit who empowers us to be effective witnesses for

Christ. Second, our witness should start wherever we spend the most time—at home, at the office, in our community, and then extend outward into every place and culture where the Lord calls us to serve.

Action Item: Declare Jesus Openly.

In Matthew 10:32–33, Jesus told His disciples, "Therefore whoever confesses Me before men, him I will also confess before My Father who is in heaven. But whoever denies Me before men, him I will also deny before My Father who is in heaven" (NKJV). The word translated "confess" could also be translated "openly declare" or "freely speak." So Jesus' statement could be accurately rendered, "Therefore whoever openly declares Me before men, I will openly declare before My Father." Do you have any trouble talking to others about your spouse or your kids? Probably not. After all, they are an inseparable part of who you are. So why should it be any different talking about Jesus? If you have been born again, He is not only your Savior but also your most important family member. He has not only raised you from spiritual death; He has become an inseparable part of who you are. The apostle Peter said it like this: "But in your hearts set apart Christ as Lord. Always be prepared to give an answer to everyone who asks you to give the reason for the hope that you have. But do this with gentleness and respect, keeping a clear conscience, so that those who speak maliciously against your good behavior in Christ may be ashamed of their slander" (1 Peter 3:15–16).

Jesus does not command us to insert Him into every conversation we have. Rather, we are to be real and transparent with others concerning our relationship with Him. We are to give Him credit, publicly and privately, for what He has done and what He is doing in our lives. And Peter tells us to share our testimony with gentleness and respect. We are not to be aggressive, arrogant, or condescending in the way we share the gospel.

ACTIVITY 6: GO OUT AND PREACH THE GOSPEL TO EVERYONE

Jesus gave His final exhortation shortly before He ascended into heaven. Acts and the gospels of Matthew, Mark, and Luke record the event and capture different aspects of His statements. Mark wrote, "He said to them, 'Go into all the world and preach the good news to all creation'" (16:15). It could be argued that this was a specific command and mission intended only for His disciples. However, even if that were true, we could view the principle behind the command and embrace the activity as our own. The Greek word that is translated "preach" can be rendered "to formally and powerfully proclaim (as a herald)." It also can mean "to proclaim openly something that has happened." With that understanding, preaching the gospel can apply to any of us.

I have had the joy of proclaiming the realities of Jesus in countless situations and locations—to audiences as small as one and as large as a full sports arena. Whether your audience is one, ten, or ten thousand, the more intimate you become with the Lord, the more freely you will be able to preach the gospel to every creature. And as we saw earlier, our goal is not simply to preach salvation but, equally important, to lead people into discipleship by "teaching them to obey everything I have commanded you" (Matthew 28:20).

ACTIVITY 7: PREACH REPENTANCE AND FORGIVENESS OF SINS

Today you can hear sermons and read Christian books that will tell you almost everything about any topic that interests you. But they don't always match the emphasis we see in Jesus' teachings. Evangelicals often lead with "feel good" messages. I've heard people share messages with themes such as "Come to Jesus and be a better you" and "Come to Jesus and have a happier marriage, a more successful career, a happier life!" Although such themes may reflect the speaker's personal experience, you won't find Jesus making such offers. Not only is Jesus the "author and finisher of our faith" (Hebrews 12:2, NKJV), but He should also be the author and finisher of our message.

In Luke 24:46–47, Jesus told His disciples, "This is what is written: The Christ will suffer and rise from the dead on the third day, and repentance and forgiveness of sins will be preached in his name to all nations, beginning at Jerusalem." Thus, the focus of our outreach to nonbelievers must be announcing the need for repentance and the good news that forgiveness of sins is available to any who would believe the gospel and follow Christ.

However, for such a message to be relevant, the listeners must first have a clear understanding of where they stand before a holy and righteous God. They first need to realize that God is perfect in His righteousness and they are lost in their sins. Only then can they know that they need forgiveness and need to repent from their sin and self-centeredness. To this end, the apostle Paul wrote, "For all have sinned and fall short of the glory of God" (Romans 3:23). He also wrote, "The wages of sin is death, but the gift of

God is eternal life in Christ Jesus our Lord" (Romans 6:23). In Ephesians 2, Paul wrote that we were dead in sin and had no hope. Dead is dead—without any opportunity for life. And "no hope" (verse 12, KJV) means none whatsoever!

But then Paul delivered the great news of the gospel: "But God, who is rich in mercy, because of His great love with which He loved us, even when we were dead in trespasses, made us alive together with Christ" (Ephesians 2:4–5, NKJV). To effectively share the message of "repentance and forgiveness of sins…in his [Christ's] name," we must communicate the reason that repentance and forgiveness are needed.

ACTIVITY 8: SPEAK IN THE DAYLIGHT WHAT CHRIST TOLD YOU AT NIGHT

In Matthew 10, as Jesus prepared to send His disciples out to preach, He gave them a number of instructions. Then almost out of the blue, He told them, "What I tell you in the dark, speak in the daylight; what is whispered in your ear, proclaim from the roofs" (verse 27). You might wonder what those words have to do with you. Although this was a specific command given to the twelve apostles, it reveals a wonderful command and activity for us as well. For most believers, the best time to meditate on the words of Jesus is at night, after all the craziness of the day has stopped. I usually spend time reading His words on a topic from the Gospels. Without fail, not only does He talk to me through His words on the page, but I engage in a quiet two-way conversation about what He's saying to me as I read. And because I take this seriously, I often tell my wife, children, or others what Jesus revealed to me the night before. Whenever I do this, I see His words and revelation bless the hearts and minds of others. And then throughout the day, I often hear the Holy Spirit whisper Jesus' words in my ear.

This is one of the eleven ministries of the Holy Spirit that Jesus revealed in the gospel of John. In John 14:26, Jesus said, "But the Helper, the Holy Spirit, whom the Father will send in My name, He will teach you all things, and bring to your remembrance all things that I said to you" (NKJV). Sometimes His whispers are meant only for me and a particular choice I am facing. Sometimes they are meant for me to quietly share with just one person, and sometimes they are meant for me to openly proclaim in a group setting. But the spirit of what Jesus is saying is, don't squash or take lightly the promptings of the Holy Spirit. When He reveals a treasure from His Word, generally it's not just for you, but it's for the people He brings into your path as well. What He speaks to you at night, share in the daylight, and what He whispers in your ear, proclaim to others.

ACTIVITY 9: BE THE SALT OF THE EARTH

In the Sermon on the Mount, Jesus called His disciples "the salt of the earth" (Matthew 5:13). At the time of Christ, salt was an extremely valuable commodity. It provided the only means of preserving food. Salt was so important that wars were fought over it. Trade routes used for transporting salt from one place to another were called "salt roads." In America during the War of 1812, soldiers were paid with salt brine instead of money. When Jesus called His disciples "the salt of the earth," He was telling them they were of extreme worth to Him and of critical importance to the world. They were to preserve the truth about Jesus and His teachings and consequently become the preserving and purifying influence in the world.

But He didn't stop there. He went on to say, "But if the salt loses its saltiness, how can it be made salty again? It is no longer good for anything, except to be thrown out and trampled by men" (Matthew 5:13). In other words, if the day ever came that Christ's disciples no longer embraced and proclaimed the truths of the gospel, they would no longer have a preserving or purifying influence in the world. The rotting and spoilage of the world would quickly follow, and they would no longer be carrying out the activity He had given them.

So what part of this preserving work are you and I to carry out? We too can become the salt of the earth. As we discover and follow the teachings of Christ, our lives become salt, conveying His love and righteousness and their preserving power to those around us. As we learn and experience these truths, we can become broadcasters of those truths to the people we influence.

ACTIVITY 10: BE THE LIGHT OF THE WORLD

In John 8:12, Jesus said, "I am the light of the world. Whoever follows me will never walk in darkness, but will have the light of life." Without the revelation of the Person of Christ and the Word of God, we would live in a world of spiritual darkness. We would be in danger of accepting all the world's standards and values as truth. We would not come into the reality of truth until we died and came face to face with God. But Jesus is the Light of the world, and His words reveal truth about ourselves, about God, and about what He values, loves, and hates. As we walk in the path He walked before us, we will have His light in our lives, and we won't have to stumble and fall in the darkness. We will have "the light of life."

Amazingly, right after Jesus called His disciples the "salt of the earth," He called them the "light of the world." But He said this in a very different context from the one in which He made the statement about Himself (see John 8:12). He provides light so His followers won't have to walk in darkness. With His light showing us the truth, we can see and embrace His values and walk in the paths of love and righteousness that He walked. But as His disciples, we are commissioned to be lights of "good deeds" so others will see our lives and praise the Father.

Jesus said, "You are the light of the world. A city on a hill cannot be hidden. Neither do people light a lamp and put it under a bowl. Instead they put it on its stand, and it gives light to everyone in the house. In the same way, let your light shine before men, that they may see your good deeds and praise your Father in heaven" (Matthew 5:14–16). He gave this assignment to His disciples, but it also is given to us.

My two best friends apart from my wife and children are Jim Shaughnessy and Gary Smalley. For forty years Jim has been a light for my world. I watch how he lets the love of Christ flow freely out of his heart to everyone God brings him into contact with. Anytime I wonder how to let Jesus' love flow through me, I need only to think of Jim and how I've seen him love others— from his own family to complete strangers. And when it comes to dealing with adversity or trials, I need only to think of the times I've seen Gary Smalley respond to trials and adversity. His life is another light in my world. Every time I think of either of these men and their examples, my heart praises our Heavenly Father.

That is exactly what Jesus has commissioned you and me to

be. Our words are critically important in reaching and blessing others, but they are not nearly as important as the light we provide by doing acts of love and righteousness that reflect the light of God's Son.

CHAPTER 12

ROADBLOCKS, BOOBY TRAPS, AND DEADLY DETOURS TO FOLLOWING CHRIST

"With men this is impossible, but with God, all things are possible."

We have clear instructions from Christ on how to have an intimate relationship with Him and the Father and how to follow Him by pursuing the four missions He gave us. We have now looked at the full meaning of being born again and read the incredible stories in the New Testament of two people who met Jesus and were born again.

Unfortunately, the New Testament is also replete with examples of those who came face to face with Jesus and yet were *not* born again. They remained dead in their sins even though the Bread of Life was only an arm's length away. They remained spiritually blind even though their eyes beheld the Light of the world. They had an opportunity to come to Christ, but their hearts remained stubbornly closed to Him and His message. When we look at the obstacles they faced, we see they are the same roadblocks and distractions standing in the way of many people today.

Can a sovereign God remove the obstacles? Absolutely! But it's important to see what they are so we can pray that they will not divert us from following Him. We also need to pray for others whose hearts are ensnared. The most common traps and obstacles frequently go unnoticed, and when they are seen, they may seem harmless. Yet they can have a deadly outcome.

There is a second reason we need to be aware of the traps. They not only stand between people and the second birth, but they can also keep those who are born again from becoming more intimate with God, from growing in maturity in Christ, and from accomplishing the missions that Jesus gave His followers. We can all fall victim to the same deadly traps.

Six obstacles stand out as the most common roadblocks that keep people from responding to God's grace or, once they are born again, prevent them from growing in spiritual maturity. Heading the list is pride, by far the greatest obstacle that blinds people to the kingdom of God and detours believers from the path that leads to the intimacy with God that He desires.

OBSTACLE 1: PRIDE

Pride is the ultimate roadblock to being born again and experiencing true intimacy with the Father and the Son. During a 1957 evangelistic crusade in New York City, Billy Graham proclaimed that nothing keeps more people out of the kingdom of God than pride. It is deadly to nonbelievers, blinding them to a vision of the one true God and His truth. Pride also inflicts damage on believers, preventing an intimate relationship with God.

When the Pharisees grilled the young man whose blindness Jesus healed, their pride and self-righteousness were obvious. They said, "You were steeped in sin at birth; how dare you lecture us!" (John 9:34), implying that they were not born in sin. They believed that they were far more righteous than the formerly blind man. In reality, their pride and self-righteousness were the problems that left them spiritually blind, and unlike the young man, they would not allow their eyes to be opened.

Pride and self-righteousness blind us to reality, to the Lord, and to His commands and promises. Pride can easily keep us living in darkness even when we think we are living in the light. Jesus said, "I tell you the truth, unless you change and become like little children, you will never enter the kingdom of heaven. Therefore, whoever humbles himself like this child is the greatest in the kingdom of heaven" (Matthew 18:3–4). Children are dependent on others to meet their needs. They took Christ at His word, believing what He said and acting on those beliefs. The reason we must become like children is that we must see that we are spiritually broke. On our own, we have no resources to remedy our spiritual bankruptcy. So we must exercise faith, take God at His word, and become totally dependent on Him to meet our spiritual needs.

The basis of genuine humility is seeing ourselves as God sees us and seeing Him as He really is. When those visions become our reality, we become aware that all that we have is because of God's grace and what He and others have given to us. Paul said it this way: "For who makes you different from anyone else? What do you have that you did not receive? And if you did receive it, why do you boast as though you did not?" (1 Corinthians 4:7). As believers, we must always realize that "God resists the proud, but gives grace to the humble" (1 Peter 5:5, NKJV). Do you want God to resist you, or do you want His grace? If it's grace that you want, then Peter tells you, "Therefore humble yourselves under the mighty hand of God, that He may exalt you in due time" (1 Peter 5:6, NKJV).

OBSTACLE 2: SELF-RIGHTEOUSNESS

This booby trap springs up and surprises its victims. If pride is the number-one obstacle to coming to know God and His grace, growing spiritually, and pursuing the missions Christ gave us, then self-righteousness is a close second. All of us can find merit in our own behavior. We can always find someone whose life is "less righteous," which gives us a false sense of goodness. "I believe in God, pray, and go to church. That's a lot better than most of the people I know." "I may not be Mother Teresa, but I'm basically a good person."

The Gallup organization stated that 81 percent of American adults believe in heaven.[3] And if the survey had asked, the researchers would have found that most of those people also think they are going to heaven. They think that, although they're not perfect, they are a lot better than most. So they are comfortable with where they are in relation to good and evil, God and the devil, heaven and hell.

For most people a mistaken belief in their own righteousness rests on four deadly errors in judgment. First, they misjudge who God is and how He acts. Second, they misjudge themselves, minimizing the reality of their sin and its deadly consequences. (At the same time they magnify their own goodness.) Third, they don't understand that God has provided only one way for sinners (which includes all of us) to get into heaven. And finally, they don't understand who Jesus is, what He said, what He offers, and what He demands of us.

Four wrong judgments feed self-righteousness. It is important to understand each error in judgment, because these wrong judgments cause most people to rely on themselves and prevent them from trusting God for eternal life. Each of the four has deadly consequences.

1. Misjudgments About Who God Is and How He Acts

Error: Because God loves us, He won't condemn anyone except people who are really bad.

Truth: God does not conform to our opinions, hopes, or preferences. He defines His own nature and character, and His dealings with humanity emanate from His nature. This is crucial, because it is impossible for God to violate His character.

God defines Himself by three attributes: His love, His righteousness, and His justice or judgment (see Jeremiah 9:24). None of these three can cancel out or violate the others. God hates sin and loves righteousness. His justice requires that He punish sin and reward righteousness. His love causes Him to extend His grace and mercy to unrighteous humanity. In light of our sin and God's unchangeable character, God can only extend His grace and mercy to us in a way that does not violate His righteousness and justice.

There was only one just and righteous solution to our sin—a substitute who would receive all the punishment that we deserve.

But that substitute would have to be Someone who had never sinned; this had to be a perfect sacrifice. The only way for this to happen was for God to send His own Son to earth to be the sacrifice.

2. Misjudgments About Our Own Goodness

Error: I am basically a good person, and I know a lot of people who are a lot worse than I am.

Truth: Have you ever been angry? Have you ever been envious? Have you ever had a lustful thought about someone other than your spouse? If so, you do not meet God's standard for "goodness."

Goodness is not a relative term. Neither is it a virtue that is graded on a curve. God sets the standard according to His nature and character, and no human has ever made the grade. Have you ever had a day when you failed to love God with all your heart, mind, soul, and strength? Have you ever failed to love your neighbor in the same way you love yourself? If you are guilty of any of these things, you are guilty of violating God's moral laws. And His righteousness and justice demand that you die spiritually. According to Jesus, you and I and everyone else have broken God's greatest laws and must pay the eternal consequences of our disobedience. God said that even when we are at our best, our actions are like filthy rags compared to His righteousness.

As we learned earlier, we don't rise higher on the scale when other people mess up more than we do. God has only one standard, and it applies to every person. He compares our values, words, actions, behavior, thoughts, and motives to His perfect righteousness—and by that standard we fall woefully short.

Without the atoning sacrifice of Jesus Christ, we would have no hope of making it into heaven.

3. Errors of Judgment Regarding God's Path to Heaven

Error: Surely there are many paths to heaven, and as long as we are good and try to do our best, we will be on a path that leads to eternal life.

Truth: Jesus said, "I am the way, the truth, and the life. No one comes to the Father except through Me" (John 14:6, NKJV).

Only two paths are available, and they lead to opposite destinations. "Enter through the narrow gate," Jesus said. "For wide is the gate and broad is the road that leads to destruction, and many enter through it. But small is the gate and narrow the road that leads to life, and only a few find it" (Matthew 7:13–14). People who follow the wide path to destruction will spend eternity separated from God, but those who find the narrow path will spend eternity in heaven with God. The wide path is a crowded road, and most people remain on it throughout life. The second road is more like a narrow footpath, able to accommodate people only if they walk single file. According to Jesus, most people don't choose that path.

The narrow path is the life of following Jesus, discovering what He said, and obeying His teachings. He restated the contrast of the two paths by using a second analogy. He said there are only two foundations on which you can build your life: one is rock; the other is sand. Lives built on the rock will be secure, and those people will enter heaven. But lives built on sand will collapse, and those people will spend eternity cut off from God. As we have seen, Jesus said the foundation of rock is hearing His words and doing them, and the unstable sand is hearing His words and not doing them (see Matthew 7:24–27).

4. Errors in Judgment Regarding Who Jesus Is, What He Said, What He Offers, and What He Demands

Error: Jesus was a Gandhi-like or Mother Teresa–like figure who walked around teaching about peace and alleviating human suffering. He offers heaven to everyone and demands nothing in return.

Truth: Jesus came to earth to accomplish twenty-seven specific missions. He made more than nineteen hundred statements that are recorded, which we can study and live by. He did not come to preach peace or alleviate human suffering. He came to reveal the truth about God the Father, Himself, eternal life, and His kingdom.

He came to earth to live a sinless life and sacrifice Himself as a full payment for the sins of all who would place their faith in Him. This faith is evidenced by a life of discovering and following His teachings and commands. He said that He calls His sheep, they hear His voice, and they follow Him. He gives them eternal life, but He offers no hope to anyone who doesn't follow Him. Like the Father, Jesus is a God of righteousness and justice as well as a God of love.

OBSTACLE 3: RELIGIOUS ACTIVITY AND TRADITION

How could the most religious people on the planet miss their own Messiah? The Pharisees met a man born blind who was healed by Jesus. They heard about hundreds of other miracles, things that had never been seen in the history of their religion. Jesus was fulfilling scores of prophesies from the Pharisees' most sacred scriptures. But did they rejoice? Did they sit at the feet of this miracle-working Rabbi and feast on His teachings? No, they attacked Him because He violated their traditions! It sounds like insanity, but it is a prime example of the blinding power of religion. Their man-made traditions blinded them to the presence of their own Messiah!

The Pharisees were not only the most religious group in Jesus' day; they may well have been the most religious people of all time. They studied the Scriptures for hours every day. They were careful to obey the letter of the law, including hundreds of Israel's civil, social, and ceremonial laws. And yet their devotion to religious activity blinded them to the truth. Jesus referred to them as the blind leading the blind (see Matthew 15:14) and as "whitewashed tombs" (Matthew 23:27). They looked clean on the outside but were full of death on the inside.

Jesus told them, "You diligently study the Scriptures because you think that by them you possess eternal life. These are the Scriptures that testify about me, yet you refuse to come to me to have life" (John 5:39–40). "Thus you nullify the word of God for the sake of your tradition. You hypocrites! Isaiah was right when he prophesied about you: 'These people honor me with their lips, but their hearts are far from me. They worship me in vain; their teachings are but rules taught by men'" (Matthew 15:6–9). Jesus repeatedly called them hypocrites, and in Luke 16:15, He summed it up with "You are the ones who justify yourselves in the eyes of men, but God knows your hearts. What is highly valued among men is detestable in God's sight."

Today, religion is more widespread than at any other time in history. We have thousands of denominations and more mega-churches than ever. People are saddled with more and more religious duties and requirements. And yet, I believe we have fewer true followers of Jesus Christ than at any time since the Reformation. We have advanced and embraced church traditions and doctrines over the direct knowledge of Jesus' words. Christians have given priority to studying subjects such as the gifts of the Holy Spirit, prophesy, the Rapture, prosperity and health, or social justice—all to the neglect of the teachings and callings of the Lord Jesus.

We have done the very thing that Jesus lambasted the Pharisees for doing—we have nullified the words of our Savior by subordinating them and even replacing them with other teachings and activities. Such things take people off the narrow path of following Christ. These professing Christians have a "form of godliness" (2 Timothy 3:5), but their lives are void of the true power of the gospel, which is exactly what Paul warned against. While many want a more intimate relationship with God, few seem to know how to achieve it. And even the most sincere believers seem less knowledgeable of the statements of Jesus than any generation of believers since the Reformation.

I'm *not* against church membership or church activities—they can be mightily used by the Holy Spirit to edify believers and proclaim the gospel. Nor am I opposed to Christians learning about prophecy or any other subject taught in the Bible. But no activity and no single subject should be allowed to overshadow the goal of gaining an intimate relationship with God—a level of intimacy that comes only by following the teachings of Jesus.

Jesus never called people to a set of religious beliefs and activities. He summed up His call in Matthew 16:24: "If anyone desires to come after Me, let him deny himself, and take up his cross, and follow Me" (NKJV). The only way we can follow Him is to discover His words and do them. We follow His words by faith, empowered by God's grace. Jesus' promises and commands are the only secure foundation upon which true faith can rest. And yet most Christians spend little time meditating on either Christ's promises or His commands. The Bread of Life is tasted by many but consumed by few. Many church members are starving spiritually.[4]

The most devastating consequence of religious distractions is that they provide a false sense of security, which will be shattered for many professing believers when they come face to face with Christ (see Matthew 7:13–23).[5] They literally produce the type of lukewarm believers described in Revelation 3:15–17.

OBSTACLE 4: WEALTH

One day a young man knelt in front of Jesus and asked, "What good thing shall I do to inherit eternal life?" When Jesus told him to keep the commandments, the man asked, "Which ones?" Jesus named six commandments, including "You shall love your neighbor as yourself" (Matthew 19:19, NKJV). The man confidently replied that he had kept all of these since his youth. He then asked, "What do I still lack?" (verse 20, NKJV). Amazingly, this man had a chance to have the most important question of his life answered by the only One who could answer it authoritatively.

Jesus' love for this young man was as great as His love for any of us. He wanted him to receive eternal life. At the same time, Jesus could not compromise the truth. Jesus told the man, "Sell everything you have and give to the poor, and you will have treasure in heaven. Then come, follow me" (Luke 18:22). How could

Jesus make such a terrible demand? The answer is simple. Like everyone else, this man could enter the kingdom of God only if he was born again. The evidence of such a new birth would be an opening of his eyes to his sin and to the surpassing greatness of Christ. His heart would turn toward repentance, and the man would do an about-face from his self-centered hoarding of wealth. He would joyfully follow the only One who could give him eternal life.

So a command from Jesus to sell everything, give it to the poor, and follow Him would be easy for a person who had been born again to obey. However, it would not be doable for anyone who sought eternal life on his own terms. This man's wealth was his god, which means he had lived in continual violation of the first of the Ten Commandments: "You shall have no other gods before Me" (Exodus 20:3, NKJV). And yet, he foolishly believed he had kept all of God's commandments. His resistance to giving his wealth away showed that he also had lived in violation of the second greatest command: "You shall love your neighbor as yourself" (Mark 12:31, NKJV). He preferred to hoard his wealth rather than use it to bless others.

Jesus had made the most incredible offer of all time! He gave this man a chance to love his neighbor as himself. He offered him the chance to put God above all the other gods in his life. And the Son of God promised that if he would do that, his treasure in heaven would be great! But the man refused Jesus' offer, because only a person who is born again would gladly trade his temporary possessions for eternal life and treasures in heaven. The young man turned and walked away. Jesus said to His disciples, "I tell you the truth, it is hard for a rich man to enter the kingdom of heaven. Again I tell you, it is easier for a camel to go through the eye of a needle than for a rich man to enter the kingdom of God" (Matthew 19:23–24). The disciples exclaimed, "Who then can be saved?" And Jesus replied, "With man this is impossible, but with God all things are possible" (verses 25–26).

It is humanly impossible to overcome the obstacle of wealth to get into the kingdom of God. But when God gives the second birth to a person, regardless of his or her wealth (or lack of it), the impossible is accomplished—not by man, but by God. This is great news for all of us in America. Every one of us is far richer than *most* of the world's population. So we are like the camel trying to pass through the eye of a needle. We can't do it unless we are truly born again. When that happens, God miraculously accomplishes the impossible.

Why is it so hard for the rich to enter God's kingdom? Because wealth can breed arrogance and a spirit of independence and the desire to be served by others. And to follow Christ, we must desire the exact opposite. We must humble ourselves, become dependent on Him, and desire to serve God and others instead of being served. Jesus said we must deny ourselves, take up our crosses, and follow Him. And until we are born again, that simply cannot happen.

OBSTACLE 5: MISPLACED VALUES

On July 16, 1999, John F. Kennedy Jr. climbed into a single-engine plane—along with his wife, Carolyn, and her sister Lauren—to fly from New Jersey to Martha's Vineyard in Massachusetts. John was still a rookie pilot, having received his pilot's license only fifteen months earlier. His wife didn't like flying with him on private planes because she didn't feel he had been flying long enough. This time, reportedly, they had disagreed over whether to fly commercial or on a private plane to a family wedding celebration. She gave in.

Once John arrived at the airport, he got the report that haze blanketed the entire New England coast. At that same New Jersey airport, another private pilot with much more experience heard the report and decided not to fly. John did not have an instrument rating or the training to fly in low visibility. He didn't worry about it, however, because he failed to recognize the degree of danger. He knew about vertigo, a condition that can develop when visibility is bad. But he didn't think it would be a problem. Besides, he wanted to get to the party sooner than a commercial airline could get him there.

Later that night he did get vertigo. He had no idea that his plane's nose was pointed down, toward the waters of the Atlantic. After he passed the red-line speed, because he had no idea how to read the instruments, he wasn't able to straighten out the aircraft. He, his wife, and her sister were killed instantly when they crashed into the choppy Atlantic.

How could this happen to such an intelligent man? Simply stated, he placed high value on what wasn't that important, and no value on what was critically important. He placed high value on getting to a party early and the ego satisfaction of flying himself. He placed no value on his wife's concerns, no value on the weather conditions, and no value on what he had learned about the dangers of not being able to identify a horizon in hazy conditions. His misplaced values cost his life and the lives of his wife and sister-in-law.

When we are born into the world, we quickly adopt the world's values, which are contrary to God's values. By the time we are confronted with the gospel, the values of the world have been deeply ingrained in our nature. We saw this in the story of the rich young ruler. He valued his possessions infinitely more than he valued the opportunity to follow the Messiah. His values were so ingrained that he couldn't break free. However, other wealthy people encountered Jesus and broke free of the world's values to embrace God's values. Of course, they had been born again. (Examples include Joseph of Arimathea, Nicodemus, and Zacchaeus.)

Zacchaeus was a chief tax collector. That meant he was rich largely because he was a cheat. Rome allowed him to keep a certain percentage of the taxes he collected. So in order to collect more, he often assessed higher taxes on people than they really owed. He not only kept his rightful percentage of the honest taxes; he also kept 100 percent of the overcharges.

One day when Jesus was passing through Jericho, the crowd around Him was so dense that Zacchaeus ran ahead and climbed a tree so he could see Jesus when He passed by. As Jesus walked down the street, He looked into the tree and said, "Zacchaeus, come down immediately. I must stay at your house today" (Luke 19:5). The tax collector came down, and Jesus went to his house. After they arrived, Zacchaeus told the Lord he was giving half of his possessions to the poor and paying back every person he had cheated, at the rate of four times the amount he had taken.

Unlike the rich young ruler, Zacchaeus and his values had been transformed. He valued his relationship with Jesus far more than he valued possessions. For all we know, paying back everyone four times the amount he had cheated them may have bankrupted him. But he didn't take time to calculate his losses; he made the commitment to do what was right.

Previously Jesus had said it was easier for a camel to pass through the eye of a needle than for a rich man to enter the kingdom of God. But to Zacchaeus He said, "Today salvation has come to this house, because he also is a son of Abraham; for the Son of Man has come to seek and to save that which was lost" (Luke 19:9–10, NKJV). The impossible had been accomplished. A rich man had been born again, and Jesus saw the evidence of new birth in Zacchaeus's heart, spirit, and behavior. He had repented and was instantly transformed from a greedy cheat to an amazingly generous philanthropist.

What do you value more than you should, and what do you fail to value as much as you should? The truth is, our values begin to change to Christ's values when we are born again and begin to have an intimate relationship with God. When we follow Christ, we discover what He said, and we start doing it. Missionary Jim Elliot followed Christ all the way into the jungles of Ecuador, taking the gospel to the most feared tribe in South America. It cost him his life at the age of twenty-nine. But before he was martyred, he had said, "He is no fool who gives what he cannot keep to gain what he cannot lose!"[6] Jim Elliot was no fool. Like Zacchaeus, his treasures in heaven are great.

OBSTACLE 6: PROCRASTINATION

Millions of people think they want to experience a closer relationship with God. Nonbelievers think, *I really need to get right with God.* And believers think, *I really want to get closer to God* or *I really want my relationship with God to become more real and intimate.* And yet, year after year they continue doing what they've always done, and time slips by with no real change taking place.

Yesterday I boarded a plane for home and sat next to a young man traveling to a business meeting. He was thirty-four years old and married with two children. He said something that hinted he was a believer, so I asked him how long he had been a Christian. He said he had accepted Christ at a young age, then lost all interest when he was in college. He had partied hard and was kicked out of college after two years. But before he left school, he fell in love with a girl he later married. One day she said, "When are we going to start attending church?" Soon they got involved in an evangelical church, and his wife committed her life to Christ. He recommitted his life to Christ as well.

But as we talked about what real intimacy with God entails, he said he was so immersed in his work and other things that he kept putting it off. However, he hoped things would change in the future. That's when I asked him a question that seemed to rattle him: "How would you feel if your children came face to face with Jesus Christ, and He told them, 'I never knew you'? Imagine if they replied, 'But Dad said that if I prayed to receive you, I would go to heaven.' And then they heard Christ say again, 'I never knew you. Depart from me!'"

I said, "Can you imagine anything worse? You say you want to work on your relationship with God, but you keep putting it off. And instead of seeing a dad who has a thriving, intimate walk with God, your children see a dad who talks about Jesus instead of following Him. How long are you going to wait before you decide to pursue a truly intimate relationship with God?"

Already he had lost ten years of experiencing the joy that Jesus longs to give. Ten years that could have resulted in miraculous spiritual growth, godliness, and power that won't be reclaimed. Ten years of setting a godly example for his wife, his children, and all who watch him (see John 15:10–11).

Have you been procrastinating in the area of being born again or of moving into greater intimacy with Christ? God is not obligated to continue extending His grace to those who ignore it day after day and year after year. In Luke 13:5, Jesus said, "Unless you repent, you too will all perish." He then told a parable in verses 6–9 that implied God will put up with those who procrastinate for only so long. When we procrastinate, we are blatantly disobeying His commands and telling Him that our desires and values are more important than His. That shows that pride controls our lives, and God has promised to resist the proud but give grace to the humble (see 1 Peter 5:5).

Jesus said to one man, " 'Follow Me.' But he said, 'Lord, let me first go and bury my father.' Jesus said to him, 'Let the dead bury their own dead, but you go and preach the kingdom of God' " (Luke 9:59–60, NKJV). This sounds callous on Jesus' part until you realize what was really being said. The statement "Let me first go and bury my father" was an accepted way of saying "Let me look after the family business and other affairs until my father dies." But Jesus said no. Telling the man to "let the dead bury their own dead, but you go and preach the kingdom of God" was Jesus' way of saying "Let others who aren't called by Me attend to your family's business. But you answer My call to follow Me right now—with no more procrastinating!" His words apply to us today.

Another person said to Jesus, " 'Lord, I will follow You, but let me first go and bid them farewell who are at my house.' But Jesus said to him, 'No one, having put his hand to the plow, and looking back, is fit for the kingdom of God' " (Luke 9:61–62, NKJV). Jesus was saying that the needs and opportunities of the present far outweigh the urge to attend to the past, even for a moment.

Procrastination is an invisible fence between you and God. It's so much a part of our nature that we are unaware of it. We intend to do what is right, as soon as we have time. But we deceive ourselves, thinking that we don't have time right now. We may fool ourselves, but we don't fool God. Stop procrastinating and start obeying His words now, while He is extending His grace to you.

Have any of these six roadblocks or distractions stood in *your* way of pursuing and achieving a more intimate relationship with God? Although all six are impossible to overcome with mere willpower or human effort, they are all easily overcome by God. In fact, Jesus has already overcome them. We don't follow Jesus a thousand miles at a time, but rather we follow Him step by step. If you follow Him by discovering and doing what He says to do, one moment at a time, He will carry you over these roadblocks with the greatest of ease. The Holy Spirit will literally reproduce the nature of Christ in you, and no roadblocks or distractions will detour you from experiencing true intimacy with God and accomplishing the missions that Jesus has set before you.

CHAPTER 13

PROMISES YOU CAN BUILD YOUR FAITH ON

*Jesus made more than a
hundred miraculous promises
to His followers.*

In 1879 thirty-year-old Russell Carter was in critical condition with a failing heart. He was told by his doctors that there was nothing else they could do for him. Carter, a professing Christian for most of his life, told the Lord that whether he recovered or not, the rest of his life would be fully consecrated to serving Him. From that time on, the Word of God became alive to Carter. He decided that no matter what his physical condition, he would believe that Christ's promises would be fulfilled in his life.

Not only did Russell survive, but within several months his heart was completely healthy. Seven years later he wrote one of my favorite hymns, "Standing on the Promises." Two of the verses are fresh in my mind:

Standing on the promises of Christ my King,
Through eternal ages let His praises ring,
Glory in the highest, I will shout and sing,
Standing on the promises of God.

Standing on the promises that cannot fail,
When the howling storms of doubt and fear assail,
By the living Word of God I shall prevail,
Standing on the promises of God.[7]

Have you ever felt like you were drowning in a howling storm of doubt and fear? I think most of us have. And yet, the promises of Christ can provide a foundation that will withstand the greatest storms that life can ever throw at you. Jesus made more than one hundred promises to His followers.[8] Most are conditional promises; Jesus set a condition that if a person obeys a particular command, *then* Jesus will deliver a promised outcome. For example, in John 6:40, He said, "Everyone who looks to the Son and believes in him shall have eternal life, and I will raise him up at the last day." The promise is twofold: eternal life and to be raised up by Christ on the last day. The conditions are that you look to the Son and believe in Him. If you look to Him alone for redemption from your sin, and you believe Him to be the Son of God, the promises will be fulfilled.[9]

Another conditional promise is stated in John 8:31–32, where we find three of the twenty promises that Jesus made about the unique role and power of His words. He said, "If you abide in My word, you are My disciples indeed. And you shall know the truth, and the truth shall make you free" (NKJV). These verses hold one condition and three promises. The three promises are that you will be one of His true disciples, you will know the absolute truth, and the truth will make you free (from enslavement to sin, see verses 34–36). The condition is that you abide (consistently reside or dwell) in His words. Conversely, if you choose not to abide in His words, then He is not obligated to deliver any of the three promises.

The truth will make you free, but the only truth that can make you free is His truth, and you will discover His truth only if you abide in His words. Furthermore, the freedom promised is not freedom from other people or freedom in a social or political sense. The freedom Jesus referred to is freedom from the enslavement to sin!

JESUS MADE MORE THAN ONE HUNDRED PROMISES TO YOU

Imagine that you are driving down a highway and you notice a car pulled off to the side of the road. A woman is struggling to change a flat tire. You pull over and offer to help—even suggesting that you'll change the tire for her. She accepts your help, then asks for your name, address, and phone number. The next day you get a call from the woman's husband, who introduces himself as Bill Gates. He gives you a computer network log-in number and says to turn on your computer and log on to Skype. You log in and key in the number, and sure enough there is Bill Gates, talking to you via a video conference. After he thanks you for helping his wife, he tells you that he's sending a package to a Microsoft office in a town about forty miles from your home. In the package will be Microsoft stock certificates worth one million dollars, and they are all yours, as long as you meet one condition.

You're all ears, ready to hear the condition. He says you should write it down, because if you fail to meet all the terms, you'll forfeit the stocks worth a million dollars. He instructs you, "Be at office number 201 at exactly noon on Friday. See Mrs. McMillan and give her the password 'blue moon 719912A.' She will ask to see your driver's license, and then she will hand you the package. If you arrive at 12:01, or if you misstate the password by even a single digit, she will not give you the package."

How closely would you follow his instructions? Pretty closely, really closely, or perfectly? You know in advance that anything less than perfect compliance will cost you one million dollars.

The conditional promises Jesus has made to you offer benefits that are infinitely greater than financial wealth. His promised benefits include eternal life, avoidance of eternal judgment, becoming a member of His family, intimacy with God, the ultimate in joy and peace, living in the continual presence of Christ and God the Father, experiencing miracles, being cleansed from sin, and seeing your life produce eternal fruit. And these are just a few of the riches He promises. But nearly every promise He made comes with a condition.

So the question becomes, if you would follow Bill Gates's conditions to receive a million dollars, why aren't you devoting your life to discovering and following Christ's conditions to see His promises become reality in your life?

You might be wondering why Christ's promises are conditional when God's love is said to be unconditional and eternal life is a free gift. Eternal life *is* free in the sense that you don't have to pay its cost. But it is available to you *only* at an incalculable cost, which God Himself paid with the sacrifice of His Son. And for you, eternal life *is* conditional in that you can experience it only by receiving it from Him. The only way you can receive it is to believe in God's Son—and believe according to Christ's definition of belief.

Further, God's love is unconditional in that He provides it every day. He could have justifiably destroyed humanity after Adam's sin, but instead He continued to show His mercy and grace to the undeserving human race. Of course the greatest act of unconditional love that humanity has witnessed was the sacrifice of God's Son. If you had been the only person who ever lived, He still would have made that sacrifice for you!

According to Jesus, the only way you can receive eternal life is by faith. So while God's love and eternal life and all His promises are freely offered, you can receive them only according to His instructions and conditions.

If we were to categorize Jesus' one-hundred-plus promises, they would fall into more than twenty-four categories. But here I will give only a small sampling of His promises. We will talk about how to amplify them and apply them to your life. I have categorized a few of the promises, and in the first category I'll give you examples of amplifying them. You can do the same type of amplification with any or all the promises He has made to you.

CHRIST'S PROMISES ABOUT ETERNAL LIFE

Most assuredly, I say to you, he who hears My word and believes in Him who sent Me has everlasting life, and shall not come into judgment, but has passed from death into life. (John 5:24, NKJV)

I am the resurrection and the life. He who believes in me will live, even though he dies. (John 11:25)

Not everyone who says to me, "Lord, Lord," will enter the kingdom of heaven, but only he who does the will of my Father who is in heaven. (Matthew 7:21)

Whoever acknowledges me before men, I will also acknowledge him before my Father in heaven. (Matthew 10:32)

But love your enemies, do good to them, and lend to them without expecting to get anything back. Then your reward will be great, and you will be sons of the Most High, because he is kind to the ungrateful and wicked. (Luke 6:35)

Examples of Amplifying Jesus' Promises About Eternal Life

In the following examples, the conditions are underlined, and the promises are italicized.

He who hears My word and believes in Him who sent Me *has everlasting life,* and *shall not come into judgment,* but *has passed from death into life.* (John 5:24, NKJV)

This verse contains two conditions and three incredible promises. The conditions are (1) we must hear Jesus' word, and (2) we must believe (*pisteuo*) in God the Father and that He sent Jesus. If we meet those two conditions, then He promises (1) that we have (right now) eternal life, (2) that we will not have to experience the terrifying judgment of God, and (3) that we have instantly been resurrected from a spiritually dead state to have a living spirit, alive and responsive to God. Amazing! Dead people made alive, given eternal life, and spared the condemning judgment of God! If you do not live in daily celebration of these amazing truths, then you do not understand how great the miracle of your salvation is. But remember that these promises are made only to the person who has heard Jesus' word or teaching and who has a consuming faith in God and the Son whom He sent.

> He who <u>believes in me</u> *will live, even though he dies.*
> (John 11:25)

The condition is believe [*pisteuo*] in Jesus. The promise is even though you will die, you will live. Over and over again, Jesus answered the greatest question of the ages by assuring us that there is life after death, which is promised to all who truly believe in Him.

> Not everyone who says to me, "Lord, Lord," will *enter the kingdom of heaven,* but <u>only he who does the will of my Father who is in heaven.</u> (Matthew 7:21)

Jesus promises eternal life, but the promise applies to one group only—those who do God's will. This might raise a question. Do we receive eternal life by hearing Jesus' word and believing in the Father who sent Him, or by believing in Jesus, or by doing the will of the Father? The answer is "all of the above." All three verses (John 5:24, John 11:25, and Matthew 7:21) describe the same glorious salvation. But each verse pictures it in a different dimension.

The person who hears Jesus' word and believes in the Father who sent Him will produce a lifetime of actively doing the Father's will, because he or she truly believes in Jesus. In contrast, a person who has a superficial belief in Christ and the Father does not have the kind of faith Jesus is talking about. That person's life will not be characterized by doing the Father's will, and that person will not enter the kingdom of heaven. Doing what Jesus teaches and commands is the expressed will of the Father. James (the half brother of Jesus) wrote, "But wilt thou know, O vain man, that faith without works is dead?" (James 2:20, KJV). Said another way, *pisteuo* faith can't help but express itself. So faith that is entirely private and invisible to the outside world is something other than biblical faith.

More of Jesus' promises follow. Choose a few of them, and see if you can amplify the meaning. In each verse underline the condition(s) and circle the promises, then write out how you can apply the conditions and promises to your life and to the circumstances you face.

Promises About Personal Fulfillment

Whoever drinks the water I give him will never thirst. Indeed, the water I give him will become in him a spring of water welling up to eternal life. (John 4:14)

Whoever believes in me, as the Scripture has said, streams of living water will flow from within him. (John 7:38)

I am the gate; whoever enters through me will be saved. He will come in and go out, and find pasture. (John 10:9)

If you obey my commands, you will remain in my love, just as I have obeyed my Father's commands and remain in his love. I have told you this so that my joy may be in you and that your joy may be complete. (John 15:10–11)

Blessed are those who hunger and thirst for righteousness, for they will be filled. Blessed are the merciful, for they will be shown mercy. (Matthew 5:6–7)

But seek first his kingdom and his righteousness, and all these things will be given to you as well. (Matthew 6:33)

Come to me, all you who are weary and burdened, and I will give you rest. (Matthew 11:28)

PROMISES ABOUT SECURITY

Therefore everyone who hears these words of mine and puts them into practice is like a wise man who built his house on the rock. The rain came down, the streams rose, and the winds blew and beat against that house; yet it did not fall, because it had its foundation on the rock. (Matthew 7:24–25)

All that the Father gives me will come to me, and whoever comes to me I will never drive away. (John 6:37)

My sheep listen to my voice; I know them, and they follow me. I give them eternal life, and they shall never perish; no one can snatch them out of my hand. (John 10:27–28)

PROMISES ABOUT INTIMACY WITH GOD

Whoever has my commands and obeys them, he is the one who loves me. He who loves me will be loved by my Father, and I too will love him and show myself to him. (John 14:21)

If anyone loves me, he will obey my teaching. My Father will love him, and we will come to him and make our home with him. (John 14:23)

If you obey my commands, you will remain in my love, just as I have obeyed my Father's commands and remain in his love. (John 15:10)

If a man remains in me and I in him, he will bear much fruit; apart from me you can do nothing. (John 15:5)

PROMISES ABOUT TRUTH AND RIGHTEOUSNESS

I am the light of the world. Whoever follows me will never walk in darkness, but will have the light of life. (John 8:12)

If you abide in My word,...you shall know the truth, and the truth shall make you free. (John 8:31–32, NKJV)

I have come into the world as a light, so that no one who believes in me should stay in darkness. (John 12:46)

PROMISES ABOUT DISCIPLESHIP

To the Jews who had believed him, Jesus said, "If you hold to my teaching, you are really my disciples. Then you will know the truth, and the truth will set you free." (John 8:31–32)

Whoever serves me must follow me; and where I am, my servant also will be. My Father will honor the one who serves me. (John 12:26)

And everyone who has left houses or brothers or sisters or father or mother or children or fields for my sake will receive a hundred times as much and will inherit eternal life. (Matthew 19:29)

PROMISES ABOUT PRAYER

And I will do whatever you ask in my name, so that the Son may bring glory to the Father. You may ask me for anything in my name, and I will do it. (John 14:13–14)

You did not choose me, but I chose you and appointed you to go and bear fruit—fruit that will last. Then the Father will give you whatever you ask in my name. (John 15:16)

In that day you will no longer ask me anything. I tell you the truth, my Father will give you whatever you ask in my name. Until now you have not asked for anything in my name. Ask and you will receive, and your joy will be complete. (John 16:23–24)

For where two or three come together in my name, there am I with them. (Matthew 18:20)

Promises About the Holy Spirit

But the Counselor, the Holy Spirit, whom the Father will send in my name, will teach you all things and will remind you of everything I have said to you. (John 14:26)

But when he, the Spirit of truth, comes, he will guide you into all truth. He will not speak on his own; he will speak only what he hears, and he will tell you what is yet to come. (John 16:13)

If you then, though you are evil, know how to give good gifts to your children, how much more will your Father in heaven give the Holy Spirit to those who ask him! (Luke 11:13)

You Have Had Only a Taste!

We have looked at fewer than half of the more than one hundred promises Jesus made to His followers. And the ones we haven't looked at are just as glorious as these. One more reminder: you can find the complete list of Jesus' promises on pages 298–304 of *The Greatest Words Ever Spoken*.

PART 3

What You Never Knew About Jesus That Will Change Your Life

CHAPTER 14

WHO *WAS* THAT MAN?

You can't follow Jesus
if you are not sure
about who He is.

When I was growing up in the 1950s, one of my childhood heroes was the cowboy of cowboys, the Lone Ranger. He was part of a group of Texas Rangers who had been ambushed. All but one of the rangers were killed. The Lone Ranger was wounded and left for dead, but he was saved by an Indian named Tonto.

The lawman recovered and decided to conceal his identity by wearing a mask. For years he and Tonto would show up in a town to clear out the lawbreakers and villains. At the end of each episode, the Lone Ranger would ride off a short distance on his trusty horse, Silver, and come to a stop. At that moment one townsman would ask another, "Who was that masked man?" The other townsman would answer, "Why, that was the Lone Ranger!" Silver would rear and lift one front leg, and the "William Tell

Overture" would begin. Then the Lone Ranger would shout to his horse, "Hi ho, Silver!" and off they would ride.

I watched dozens of episodes, but I never did find out the Lone Ranger's true identity. I couldn't help but wonder about him. What was his real name? Who was the Lone Ranger? That mystery was never solved, but the identity of Jesus Christ has never been in question. We can know with absolute certainty His true identity, why He came to earth, and what His answers are to every issue we will ever face.

A skeptic would quickly say, "You can't really *know*. You can only hope or believe." I would answer, "You are wrong. And before this book ends, you too will know who Jesus is beyond any doubt."

WHO IS JESUS?

Let's start with the question of *who*. We can know who Jesus was beyond any shadow of doubt for six reasons.

1. He *told* us who He was.
2. His *actions* proved that He was telling the truth.
3. The *response* of His first-century followers proved His identity claims to be true.
4. Jesus rose from the depths of obscurity to have an *unparalleled impact* on the world, showing that he was no mere human.
5. An undeniable *mathematical proof* proves that Jesus was the Messiah.
6. The *logical argument* that J. R. R. Tolkien used with C. S. Lewis proves that Jesus was the divine Being He claimed to be.

1. HE TOLD US WHO HE WAS

Jesus told us who He was. He made more than 170 claims to divinity. Only God in human flesh could make these claims and back them up. In a handful of the claims, He made it clear where He came from. Imagine what people would say if you or I made such preposterous claims. The difference with Jesus is that He lived out every claim He made, including the statement "I and My Father are one" (John 10:30, NKJV).

His Stated Identity

Consider Jesus' claims to deity. He claimed:

1. He is the one and only Son of God (see John 3:16; Matthew 16:16–17; Luke 22:70).
2. He was sent to earth by God the Father (see John 6:38).
3. He is the only One who has come from heaven to earth (see John 3:13; 6:38, 41).
4. He was the only One who had seen the Father (see John 6:46).
5. He is the eternal "I AM" of the Old Testament (see John 8:58; Exodus 3:14).
6. He is in perfect unity or oneness with God the Father (see John 10:30).
7. He is the Messiah, the Holy One of God (see John 4:26; 6:69; Matthew 26:24).
8. He is the King of the kingdom of heaven (see John 18:36).
9. He is the Teacher of ultimate truth (see Matthew 23:10).
10. He is the Way, the Truth, and the Life and the only Way to God (see John 14:6).

11. He is the Light of the world (see John 8:12).

12. He is the Bread of Life (see John 6:48–51).

13. He is the eternal Judge of all humanity (see John 5:22, 27).

14. He is the Gift of God (see John 3:16; 4:10).

15. He is the Giver of eternal life (see John 10:27–28).

16. He is King of the Jews (see Matthew 27:11).

17. He is the Alpha and Omega, the Beginning and the End (see Revelation 22:13).

2. HIS ACTIONS PROVED HE WAS TELLING THE TRUTH

The actions of Jesus, recorded in great detail in the Gospels, proved He was telling the truth. If you or I tried to convince people we were the one and only son or daughter of God, no one would take us seriously. And yet, in Jesus' case the opposite was true. We are told that all who heard Him teach, from the educated and noble to the lowliest of commoners, were "astonished" by His words and the authority with which He taught (see Matthew 7:28; 13:54, NKJV). And backing up His words were His actions.

Jesus performed hundreds of miracles that spoke louder than words—miracles that were witnessed by thousands of people. Throughout the first and second centuries, even His detractors did not deny His miracles; there were too many witnesses who knew what they had seen. So rather than deny His miracles, Jesus' enemies attributed His miracles to sorcery or demonic possession or to Satan himself. Even Josephus, the most renowned first-century Jewish historian, acknowledged that Jesus was a teacher and "miracle worker" with a large following that continued long after He died.[10]

People can claim to be anything they imagine, but only those who back up their claims with corresponding behavior are taken seriously. Let's face it, if you saw someone give sight to the blind, feed thousands of people with a few small fish and a little bread, walk on water, and bring a rotten corpse back to life, you too would have to take that person seriously.

3. THE RESPONSE OF HIS DISCIPLES AND OTHER FIRST-CENTURY FOLLOWERS

The actions, testimonies, and lives of Jesus' original disciples and His other first-century followers proved His identity claims to be true. Would you give up everything you own and leave the family you love to perpetuate a story that you knew to be a lie? Would you endure horrible torture and an agonizing death to perpetuate a lie, especially when the lie offered you no earthly gain? Would you put your family at risk of being tortured and even executed for the sake of a preposterous story that you knew to be a hoax? Of course not!

A single insane person, acting alone, might die for a lie and subject his family to suffering for that lie. But would eleven men insist on preaching a lie when they knew they would be persecuted for it? How about thousands of people? And yet, ten of Jesus' first disciples, along with the apostle Paul and thousands of other first-century believers, chose torture and death rather than deny what they knew to be true—that Jesus had risen from the dead.

Can you imagine the eleven apostles conspiring to steal Jesus' body from the tomb so they could stage a false resurrection? Imagine Peter doing such a thing. (Remember, he was the cowardly disciple who, on the night of Jesus' arrest, denied three times that he even knew Christ.) Peter would never concoct an elaborate hoax just to fool people into believing that Jesus rose from the dead.

Just imagine Peter telling the other disciples who had also fled for their lives, "Okay, guys, we're going to rush the heavily armed Roman soldiers who are guarding His tomb. After we subdue them, we'll roll away the giant boulder that seals the tomb. Then we're going to steal Jesus' body and bury it where no one will ever find it. Then we'll wait forty days, and on the day of Pentecost, we'll go out and tell the people who demanded Jesus' crucifixion that they murdered their own Messiah. After that, we'll spend the rest of our lives running from all those who want to kill us. But while we're hiding and moving on to different areas to stay alive, we'll keep telling our story that Jesus rose from the dead. And by the way, when the authorities finally catch us, we will refuse to change our story, even when they are nailing us to a cross or cutting us in half or exiling us to an island. And, guys, realize that we're never going to make a dime doing all this, and most people are going to hate us. But that's okay. The myth we're going to create will be worth all the trouble."

As ludicrous as this is, it's not far from the type of scenario that skeptics have advanced for nearly two thousand years.

The truth is, the apostles and other witnesses of Christ's resurrection and postdeath appearances had no motive to lie. They never pursued wealth, comfort, or fame. By proclaiming Jesus' resurrection, they made themselves hated enemies of the state.

Even in the final minutes before their executions, when offered a pardon if they would deny their Savior, not one would recant. A person who is ignorant of first-century history might say, "All of this is based on New Testament writings that are nothing more than a collection of myths. They were circulated to a bunch of uneducated peasants, who then became believers in those myths." Nothing could be further from the truth. More than twenty thousand copies of the gospel writings were created by hand and circulated between the time of Christ's death and the end of the first century, about seventy years later. These copies were not circulated among only the uninformed and naive gentiles. They also were embraced by thousands of Jews who had witnessed firsthand Jesus' life and teachings, His own miracles, and the miracles performed by the apostles. It is ludicrous to think that these people would become part of this unpopular sect, which was condemned by leaders of the temple, if they knew it to be untrue. Jews who followed Jesus sacrificed family ties, their wealth, and even their lives to bear witness to Christ.

It would be like my writing a book about the terrorist attacks of September 11, 2001. But instead of describing the commercial airliners that crashed into the Pentagon and the World Trade Center, I would write about an earthquake that wrought all the destruction. Who would buy such a book, much less believe it? There are too many people alive who witnessed the planes flying into the towers. Trying to advance any other story in this generation would be fruitless.

This is the situation that existed in the first century. It has been estimated that the first sixty thousand followers of Christ were Jews and Samaritans, most of whom were either firsthand witnesses of Christ and the apostolic miracles or children of such witnesses. Myths circulated to those people would never have gained any traction. And the testimonies of firsthand witnesses are authentic and powerful, so powerful that more than one million people became followers of Christ before the end of that century (approximately seventy years after Jesus' resurrection).

4. HIS UNPARALLELED IMPACT ON THE WORLD FROM THE DEPTHS OF OBSCURITY

In today's world even a minor event occurring in a remote part of the world can become known worldwide in a matter of seconds. This makes it hard for us to imagine a world without mass communication. But when Jesus lived on earth, information was passed on by word of mouth, public proclamation, or in handwritten manuscripts (although paper had not yet been invented).

And when it came to transportation, the situation was no better. For most of the population, transportation was limited to walking. A few had access to horses, mules, or ships. Consequently, even news of major wars took months to reach the population of a nation or empire. It was in this world that Jesus was born to a peasant couple in a village in the middle of nowhere. He lived in a country occupied by foreign conquerors. His only means of transportation were his legs and an occasional boat.

He was a carpenter until He turned thirty, and only then did He begin to teach and speak in public. For three years He proclaimed His message mostly in small villages but occasionally in Jerusalem. He never ventured more than two hundred miles from the place of His birth. Then, at age thirty-three, He was arrested, falsely accused, and convicted in a rigged trial. He was sentenced to death by a Roman official, even though that official believed

Jesus to be innocent of any wrongdoing. Executed on a cross between two criminals, Jesus died the torturous death that normally was limited to murderers or proven enemies of Rome. He was surrounded by a hateful, jeering mob. Of all who had followed Him, only His mother and a few of His followers were present at the scene of His execution. All but one of His disciples had fled for their lives.

It was only after Jesus rose from the dead and appeared to His followers that His disciples were transformed from cowards into confident, fearless believers and preachers of His message. But even then they had no means to spread His teachings to mass audiences. Their audiences were limited in size by the range of their voices and the laborious process of writing on papyrus scrolls.

Given the limitations of first-century technology, it is almost inconceivable that Jesus' story spread beyond Palestine. On top of everything else, only thirty-six years after He died, Rome's military legions reduced Jerusalem to a pile of rubble. Its inhabitants (Jews and Christian Jews alike) were scattered throughout the known world with no country of their own. Given this history, you can begin to understand the miracle of the vast reach of Jesus' life story and teachings. Far from being lost to future generations, Jesus' short earthly life became the *focal point* of history.

How could one man's life impact humanity more than any other person, group of people, or series of events? Jesus did it all without money, armies, science, or political power. He did it with only the witness of His life and the power of His words. Though the miracles He performed attracted attention and gave credibility to His claims, it was what He said that melted people's hearts and transformed their lives. The apostle John summed it up: "The Word became flesh and dwelt among us, and we beheld His glory, the glory as of the only begotten of the Father, full of grace and truth" (John 1:14, NKJV).

5. MATHEMATICS PROVES THAT JESUS WAS THE PROPHESIED JEWISH MESSIAH

An unparalleled mathematical proof shows that Jesus was the prophesied Messiah. In His brief life, Jesus fulfilled hundreds of Old Testament prophesies that described the birth, life, and death of the Jewish Messiah. Mathematics professors Peter W. Stoner and Robert C. Newman, with PhDs from M.I.T. in mathematics and astrophysics, calculated the statistical probability of one person during one lifetime fulfilling just forty-eight of the highly detailed prophesies. The odds turned out to be 1 chance in 10 to the 157th power.[11] That's a 1 in 10,000,000,000,000,000,000,000, 000,000,000,000,000,000,000,000,000,000,000,000,000,000, 000,000,000,000,000,000,000,000,000,000,000,000,000,000, 000,000,000,000,000,000,000,000,000,000,000,000,000,000, 000,000,000 chance.

To put this number in perspective, let's say you built a wooden box so big that the solar system would fit inside it. And then you filled the box with silver BBs and placed just one copper BB somewhere in the box. The chances of anyone reaching into the box and picking out the copper BB on his or her first try would be trillions of times more likely than the odds of one person fulfilling even forty-eight of the prophecies that Jesus fulfilled. There is no occurrence in history or physical science that beats odds that are even close to these. In other words, nothing else has been verified with a higher degree of statistical certainty than the *fact* that Jesus is exactly who He claimed to be—the Messiah, the Son of the living God.

Some two thousand years after Jesus' execution, all this evidence works together to back up Jesus' claims about Himself.

6. THE LOGICAL ARGUMENT THAT PROVES JESUS WAS THE DIVINE BEING HE CLAIMED TO BE

An impeccable argument proves that Jesus was the divine Being He claimed to be. C. S. Lewis was chairman of the literature department at Oxford University. J. R. R. Tolkien was a tenured professor under Lewis and was Lewis's best friend. Both men were recognized as literary and philosophical geniuses. Lewis was one of England's most brilliant and articulate atheists. Tolkien was a devout Catholic whose love for Jesus Christ was known to all his peers. According to one, Tolkien asked Lewis a simple question, the answer to which shook the foundation of Lewis's atheistic beliefs. The answer changed the course of his life.

The question and the conversation were reported to have gone something like this: Tolkien asked, "Who do you think Jesus was?" Lewis answered, "A good moral man, and perhaps the greatest teacher of morality the world has ever known." Tolkien replied, "That is impossible! He could not have been just a good moral man! Look at his claims."

Tolkien recited a number of Jesus' divine claims. He said that if Jesus was not who He claimed to be, there were only two alternatives—He was either a liar or a lunatic. And not just an accidental liar or a mere eccentric. If a liar, then He would be the greatest liar who ever lived—for His lies would have deceived hundreds of millions who had placed their hopes for eternity on Him. And if a lunatic, then as Lewis later wrote, Jesus would be a lunatic "on a level with the man who says he is a poached egg."[12]

As the conversation continued, Tolkien and Lewis first looked at the possibility that Jesus was a liar—the greatest deceiver ever. As skilled philosophers, they both knew that a sane man lies for only two reasons: self-preservation or self-exaltation. He wants to preserve his life and what he has, or he wants to inflate his image, to appear to be more than he really is. Lies are told to manipulate the minds and actions of others to fulfill the liar's self-interest.

Lewis realized that this eliminated the liar alternative. Jesus never tried to preserve or protect Himself. From the beginning of His public ministry, He proclaimed that He had come to earth to die—to lay down His life. He didn't even try to prevent His own execution but rather told His disciples and His executioner that the unjust execution was part of God's plan.

Nor did He want to exalt Himself. When the crowds wanted to make Him their leader and king, He refused. Instead of exalting Himself, He gave all the credit for everything He said and did to His Heavenly Father, whom He continually exalted. When Jesus told the rich young ruler to sell everything he owned, He did not say, "And bring the money to Me, and we'll change the world." No, even though Jesus had no home and no material possessions other than the clothes on His back, He didn't want a penny. He simply told the young man, "Sell everything you have and give to the poor, and you will have treasure in heaven" (Luke 18:22). Over and over, He told His listeners that He came to glorify His Father. Conclusion: Jesus was not motivated by self-preservation or self-exaltation, so He wasn't a liar!

With the liar alternative eliminated, only two possibilities remained. Jesus was a lunatic, or He was who He claimed to be, the Son of the Living God.

A lunatic is defined by his preposterous claims or crazy behavior. If I made all the claims Jesus made, I would be committed to a mental institution. Or if you and I were standing at the edge of the Grand Canyon, and I told you I was going to jump to the other side, you would alert a park ranger, because you would know I was a lunatic. But if I stepped back fifty feet, then ran to the edge and jumped and flew five miles to the other side, I'd no longer be a lunatic. I would simply be the world's best long jumper! When someone makes preposterous claims and then backs them up with the appropriate action, that person can no longer be considered a lunatic.

The same logic applies here. Jesus didn't just claim that He had the power over life and death; He proved it by raising a man who had been dead for four days. And He did it in front of hundreds of witnesses who had been mourning the man's death. Jesus didn't just claim to be able to walk on water, turn water to wine, or feed thousands with a few fish and loaves of bread. He did all of the above. He healed the sick, gave sight to the blind, and brought more than one dead person back to life. He didn't just claim that He would raise Himself from the dead—He did it! He died in front of a huge crowd. He was determined to be dead by Roman soldiers who had seen death hundreds of times. Jesus' dead body was wrapped in burial garments and placed in a tomb that was sealed with a stone that weighed hundreds if not thousands of pounds. A squad of Roman soldiers was posted to guard against anyone stealing the body.

But the guards were mysteriously knocked out, the stone was moved, and Jesus appeared alive and well in front of hundreds of people in the days that followed. Jesus backed up His seemingly preposterous claims with the appropriate miraculous actions— actions witnessed by crowds ranging in size from hundreds to thousands. C. S. Lewis conceded the argument: Jesus could not be a lunatic.

Concluding that Jesus was neither a liar nor a lunatic, Lewis was left with only one alternative—the shocking alternative. Jesus was the Person He claimed to be, the Messiah, the Son of the Living God. And that conclusion demands a second conclusion— that there is a God. Being an honest intellectual, Lewis not only conceded the existence of God; he spent the rest of his life doing all he could to serve God and to know Him more intimately. In his book *Mere Christianity,* Lewis concludes "The Shocking Alternative" chapter with the following statement:

> I am trying here to prevent anyone saying the really foolish thing that people often say about Him: "I'm ready to accept Jesus as a great moral teacher, but I don't accept His claim to be God." That is the one thing we must not say. A man who was merely a man and said the sort of things Jesus said would not be a great moral teacher. He would either be a lunatic—on a level with the man who says he is a poached egg—or else he would be the Devil of Hell. You must make your choice. Either this man was, and is, the Son of God: or else a madman or something worse. You can shut Him up for a fool, you can spit at Him and kill Him as a demon; or you can fall at His feet and call Him Lord and God. But let us not come with any patronising nonsense about His being a great human teacher. He has not left that open to us. He did not intend to.[13]

There Can Be No Other Intellectually Honest Conclusion

Whether it's the mathematical proof devised by Stoner and Newman, the logical proof of Tolkien and Lewis, or the evidence of Christ's rise from obscurity in ancient times to impact world history more than any other person, the evidence that Jesus was the eternal Son of God cannot be logically set aside. And yet, as wonderful as these proofs are, they are not the ultimate proofs for people who have come to intimately know and experience Jesus Christ. The convincing "proofs" for those people are that He infuses hope in the midst of despair, joy when hearts are broken, and miraculous peace that subdues even the most paralyzing fears. For those of us who receive His guidance, His love and forgiveness, and His grace and power, no substitute can be found in anyone else or anything the world can offer. All else pales into insignificance.

Of all the statements I have read, the assessment by Napoleon Bonaparte comes closest to capturing Jesus' uniqueness. In addition to being the emperor of France, Napoleon is recognized as a genius and one of the greatest military strategists in history. While in exile in 1815, he stated:

> I know men; and I tell you that Jesus Christ is no mere man. Between Him and every other person in the world there is no possible term of comparison! Superficial minds see a resemblance between Christ and the founders of empires, and the gods of other religions. That resemblance does not exist.... Everything in Christ astonishes me. His spirit overawes me, and his will confounds me. He is truly

a being by Himself. His ideas and sentiments, the truth which He announces, His manner of convincing, are not explained either by human organization or by the nature of things...

The nearer I approach, the more carefully I examine, everything is above me—everything remains grand, of a grandeur which overpowers.... One can absolutely find nowhere, but in Him alone, the imitation or the example of His life... I search in vain in history to find the similar to Jesus Christ. Neither history, nor humanity, nor the ages, nor nature, offer me anything with which I am able to compare it or explain it. Here everything is extraordinary.[14]

What did Napoleon know that so many others do not? He was a student of history and a student of men. He had diligently studied the life and words of Christ. In light of this, he drew the only conclusion that someone with his degree of knowledge could draw—that Jesus was and is the Person He claimed to be.

CHAPTER 15

JESUS WAS NOT A SOCIALIST, A SANTA CLAUS, OR A RELIGIOUS LEADER

He does not give people the option of recasting Him to suit their agenda.

Jesus is a favorite subject of people who like to rewrite history, refashioning it to suit their own preferences. Various groups have adopted Jesus as an early proponent of their cause, recasting His identity in ways that support their personal worldviews or political commitments. In doing so, they reduce Him to the status of a mere human, calling Him a great teacher, an ethical leader, a prophet, or an early visionary. While pretending to honor Him with such titles, they deny His divinity and ignore the truth that He claimed equality with God.

This is not a recent phenomenon. Even while Jesus was living on earth, people speculated about His origins, His mission, and His identity. We know this because Jesus asked His disciples,

" 'Who do men say that I, the Son of Man, am?' So they said, 'Some say John the Baptist, some Elijah, and others Jeremiah or one of the prophets' " (Matthew 16:13–14, NKJV). For two thousand years, there has been no shortage of theories about Jesus. People are more than happy to remake Him in their own image and to enlist Him in support of their pet causes. As we saw earlier, these people are dead wrong. Jesus does not give anyone the option of assigning Him a new role or identity. He does invite us to accept Him and follow Him, but only on His terms.

For years my wife and I have watched *The O'Reilly Factor*. When Bill O'Reilly interviews a politician, he always welcomes the person to what he calls the No-Spin Zone. Most of the politicians he interviews try to spin their stories rather than sticking to the straight facts of the issue they are discussing. Often politicians are such talented spinners that they never get down to the reality of the issue. They answer questions with questions or by bringing up side issues—or even unrelated issues—to perpetuate their spin.

But as much spinning as people do about political issues, it's nothing compared to how they spin the truth about Jesus. People who have no personal interest in or commitment to Jesus and why He came to earth are quick to quote one of His statements out of context to make it seem to support their personal, social, cultural, or political beliefs. Unfortunately, many of these people are ministers who supposedly represent God but in reality merely represent their own views. They preach a gospel of social justice or liberation theology that has no basis whatsoever in the teachings of Jesus Christ. Yet because they wear white collars or have clerical titles attached to their names, people assume that they are followers and representatives of Christ. I've had the opportunity to meet a few such ministers, and after I've asked two or three questions, they've quickly revealed how ignorant they are of most of Jesus' statements.

Here is the most striking example. Jesus defined His true followers as those who hear His words and do them (see Matthew 7:24). By that definition, ministers who know very little of what Christ taught are no more the followers of Jesus than people who have merely read about Mount Everest are climbers of that great mountain. Knowing a little about Jesus doesn't make you one of His followers.

Common among most of these ministers and a good number of politicians is the concept that Jesus would support their efforts in the areas of entitlements and the redistribution of wealth in America. In other words, they contend that He would endorse taking the property and earnings of the haves and handing them to the have-nots, who have done nothing to merit them.

Here is the truth of the matter: Jesus' statements show His own disgust at such a practice. While He calls on all His followers to be generous beyond measure, He condemned the entitlement mentalities that were espoused in His day! At the same time, He spoke words of praise and support for those who were diligent and responsible. He taught that a person has the right to do whatever he pleases with his own property and money, with no obligation to comply with what others would consider fairness to outsiders. Jesus demonstrates this in three of His parables.

THE VINEYARD OWNER AND HIS WORKERS

In Matthew 20:1–15, Jesus shared a parable about a vineyard owner. In this story the landowner hired a group of workers at daybreak to harvest his crop. He offered to pay them a wage of one denarius for a day's labor, and they happily agreed.

At 9:00 a.m. the landowner hired another group of workers and told them he'd pay them a fair wage. They also happily agreed and quickly went to work. At noon and at 3:00 p.m., he hired two more groups and agreed to pay them a fair wage. They too immediately went to work.

Later on, at 5:00 p.m., the vineyard owner went into the town and saw a group of workers standing around. When he asked why they had remained idle all day, they replied, "Because no one hired us." Moved by compassion, the vineyard owner told them, "You also go and work in my vineyard." It appears that he hired these workers, not because he needed extra help, but because they had been there all day without work.

An hour later the owner told his supervisor to call in the workers and pay them their wages, starting with those who were hired last. To everyone's surprise, he paid those who had worked only one hour one denarius—the same amount he had promised to pay those hired first for a full day's work. This raised the expectations of the workers who had labored much longer. They reasoned that since he paid the last workers one denarius for just an hour, surely he would pay those who had worked much longer a better wage. But the vineyard owner paid all the workers the same wage—whether they had worked twelve hours or just one.

As each one received his money, the workers began to complain. They told the landowner, "These men who were hired last worked only one hour…and you have made them equal to us who have borne the burden of the work and the heat of the day." But the landowner said, "Friend, I am not being unfair to you. Didn't you agree to work for a denarius? Take your pay and go. I want to give the man who was hired last the same as I gave you. Don't I have the right to do what I want with my own money? Or are you envious because I am generous?"

Wow! Jesus tells us that a man with money has the right to do whatever he wants with it. He can be as generous as he wants, and he can be as shrewd as he wants. Liberal politicians act as if it's wrong for a person to be a shrewd and profitable businessman. They also act as if those who have money should have less control over it and have an obligation to pay higher taxes and have their wealth redistributed.

During his 2008 campaign for president, then U.S. Senator Barack Obama told "Joe the Plumber" that he wanted to "spread the wealth around." In other words, the state should have the right to take one person's money and give it to someone who hasn't worked for it. This is contrary to what Jesus said. Although this parable was intended to show that God has the right to extend His offer of mercy to any person of any nation at any time He pleases, the fact is, Jesus used the story to make His point because of its obvious logic.

Liberal politicians have said that CEOs and other corporate officers should have their wages capped and regulated by the government. They act as if it's a crime to pay a CEO millions of dollars while paying a worker only tens of thousands. Nothing could be more contrary to Jesus' teaching. In Matthew 20:12–15, Jesus teaches that people have the right to do whatever they wish with their money. If corporate shareholders want to pay high rewards to a CEO who increases the worth of their holdings, as the owners of the company, *they* have the choice to do just that.

But if this parable doesn't convince you of Jesus' anti-entitlement stance, how about two more examples?

THE PARABLE OF THE TALENTS

In the parable of the talents (see Matthew 25:14–30), Jesus told the story of a businessman who was about to go on a long journey (probably lasting more than a year). The man left his investment portfolio in the hands of three money managers. In terms of today's dollars, he divided an estimated $5.76 million among the three. He allocated the money according to the ability of each manager. The one with the greatest ability received five talents (about $3.6 million). He gave the manager with the second greatest ability two talents (about $1.44 million). The manager with the least ability received one talent (about $720,000). When the businessman returned from his journey, each manager was required to give a full accounting of his success in managing what had been entrusted to him.

The manager of the $3.6 million portfolio doubled its size to $7.2 million. The man who invested $1.44 million doubled it to $2.88 million. But the third manager buried the $720,000 in a safe place. He returned the entire amount to the owner but had realized no gain on the principal. This manager had taken no risk, made no effort, and generated no return on the investment. The two managers who doubled their investments were generously rewarded, praised, and promoted. Their reward wasn't based on how they performed as a group or in relation to one another but rather how they performed in relation to their own ability.

But the third manager, who buried what had been entrusted to him, received a very different response from the boss. That manager told his boss, "'Master, I knew that you are a hard man, harvesting where you have not sown and gathering where you have not scattered seed. So I was afraid and went out and hid your talent [money] in the ground. See, here is what belongs to you.' His master replied, 'You wicked, lazy servant! So you knew that I harvest where I have not sown and gather where I have not scattered seed? Well then, you should have put my money on deposit with the bankers, so that when I returned I would have received it back with interest.'"

The boss then told his other servants, "Take the talent [$720,000] from him [the nonproductive money manager] and give it to the one who has the ten talents. For everyone who has will be given more, and he will have an abundance. Whoever does not have, even what he has will be taken from him. And throw that worthless servant outside, into the darkness, where there will be weeping and gnashing of teeth."

So much for an entitlement mentality! This is the opposite of politically correct thinking. The managers who worked diligently weren't rewarded according to the hours they worked but rather according to their performance—their success at increasing their master's profit! The more profit they made, the greater they were rewarded. And the one whose efforts resulted in no return on investment was not only *not* rewarded but was stripped of what he had originally been given. His boss characterized him as a wicked, lazy, and worthless servant. (No political correctness there!) He was then fired and thrown into the darkness, relegated to the life of a beggar.

Why was this man treated so harshly? (See Matthew 25:26, 30.) His master had been on a long journey that most likely lasted a year or more. During that time the third money manager had received full salary plus all the food he could eat and a room in his master's house. Yet during that time he worked for only one day. He dug a hole and buried the money. Accepting a year or two of wages, room, and board for one day's work was not only lazy; it was stealing.

And here's what will surprise most people. Jesus does *not* criticize the master for rewarding success and harshly punishing laziness! Instead, His criticism is reserved solely for the nonperforming money manager. That manager thought he should be rewarded for just showing up and not losing any of the principal of the master's money. Yet, through the voice of the boss in the parable, Jesus called him lazy, wicked, and worthless!

Does this sound anything like the "Santa Claus Jesus" or the "Liberal Socialist Jesus" that many liberals and social-justice ministers portray? Hardly! While liberals say the government should take money away from those who are successful and give it to those who aren't, Jesus said the exact opposite. In His parable the boss took everything from the man who didn't produce and gave it to the money manager who was the most successful. Imagine that—letting the most successful people keep the highest percentage of their money! Jesus praised this value/reward model, while liberal politicians condemn it. Jesus and the liberals are on opposite ends of the spectrum.

Imagine an income-tax system that would reward diligence and productive performance rather than penalizing it by assessing taxes at a higher rate. The better you perform, the more you make, and the more you make, the less you are taxed. People would work harder so they could move up to a higher income, knowing they would be rewarded with a lower tax rate. Talk about turning the economy around! Even a flat tax rate would likely have the same effect.

And if you suspect I pulled a couple of Jesus' parables out of context, I'll give you one more example.

UNWORTHY SERVANTS

In Luke 17:7–10, Jesus gave this example to His disciples:

> Suppose one of you had a servant plowing or looking after the sheep. Would he say to the servant when he comes in from the field, "Come along now and sit down to eat"? Would he not rather say, "Prepare my supper, get yourself ready and wait on me while I eat and drink; after that you may eat and drink"? Would he thank the servant because he did what he was told to do? So you also, when you have done everything you were told to do, should say, "We are unworthy servants; we have only done our duty."

Jesus told His disciples that they (and we) should consider ourselves to be unworthy servants when we do *only* what we are *supposed* to do. Why? Because when we know that doing the minimum qualifies us only as unworthy workers, we will strive to do *more* than is expected. We will be motivated to excel because it will result in greater success and greater blessing.

The Greatest Servant of All

If you think Jesus' words are overly harsh, consider that He was the greatest Servant of all. He sacrificed His life in order to redeem you and me—to liberate us from the power, condemnation, and eternal consequences of our sin. He who was entitled to all of heaven's glory set aside His rights and became the greatest Servant, even to the point of a torturous death. The apostle Paul admonishes us to have the same attitude of surrendering all our rights and permanently ending our entitlement mentality (see Philippians 2:5–8).

Although Jesus demonstrated His opposition to laziness and the entitlement mentality, at the same time He called on His followers to be generous beyond measure. So while He maintained that no one had the *right* to take away what others had earned, He warned His followers to guard their hearts from all forms of greed (see Luke 12:15) and to joyfully and freely give to meet the genuine needs of others. He praised those who would freely give of themselves and their substance and harshly criticized those who would turn their backs on the needs of others (see Matthew 25:34–46; Luke 6:27–36, 38).

A RELIGIOUS LEADER? NOT!

Jesus Christ did not come to earth to start a new religion. In fact, He leveled His harshest criticism at the religious leaders of His day. He accused them of not knowing God and said they used religion to trap people in a life of misery, frustration, and failure. He claimed the religious leaders themselves were blind and had blinded the spiritual eyes of their followers (see Matthew 15:13–14; 23:13–23). He labeled those leaders as hypocrites, saying they had replaced the teachings and commands of God with commands and traditions of men (see Mark 7:6–8).

Rather than starting a new religion, Jesus claimed to be the fulfillment of all of God's moral laws that had been revealed to the seed of Abraham, the nation of Israel (see Matthew 5:17). He came to proclaim His gospel of light and truth, to Israel first and ultimately to all nations on earth. Rather than calling on people to focus on religious ceremony, He told His would-be followers and disciples: "If anyone would come after me, he must deny himself and take up his cross and follow me" (Matthew 16:24). He commanded His followers to believe that He was the Messiah sent from God, to repent (change their life's direction from one of self-centeredness to a one of doing God's will), and to be baptized as a testimony of their repentance and new commitment. At the Last Supper, He told His disciples to remember the sacrifice of His blood and body by partaking of bread and wine. And in His Great Commission, He told the disciples, "Therefore go and make disciples of all nations, baptizing them in the name of the Father and of the Son and of the Holy Spirit, and teaching them to obey everything I have commanded you" (Matthew 28:19–20).

"Wait a minute," you say. "What about His statement to Peter: 'Upon this rock I will build my church; and the gates of hell shall not prevail against it' (Matthew 16:18, KJV)? Doesn't that imply that He came to start a new religion or church?" Not really. The Greek word that is translated "church" is the word *ecclesia*. It literally means a gathering of "called-out ones." *Ecclesia* refers to any group of Jesus' followers who are called out from the peoples of all the nations to follow Him. *Ecclesia* had been used in common language for more than two hundred years before Christ and had never been used to describe a structured organization.

I am not saying that churches as we know them are not ordained or called of God. But I am saying that a church, or "the church" as Jesus referred to it, is not an organization or a building. Rather, it is a group of people who have been called out from the world to replace their self-centered values with faith in Jesus Christ as their Savior and Lord. They have a grace-powered commitment to follow Him by embracing His teachings and doing what He taught.

Unfortunately, many churches have focused on calling people to join their organization and participate in their activities in *place* of calling people to become sold-out followers of Christ. Although at times the gates of hell have prevailed against Christian organizations, they have never prevailed over the true followers of Jesus Christ, nor will they.

Jesus is the Head, the Leader of all who follow Him—those whom the apostle Paul called "the body of Christ." In that sense He is the leader of the church. However, I can promise that He would never describe Himself as the leader of a religion. Jesus' call to His followers is to listen to what He said and do it! He gave more than 140 commands and instructions to His followers, and He tells us that when we are empowered by the Holy Spirit, our faith is expressed by doing what He told us to do. We do what He says, not to earn His love or to merit eternal life, but to express our love for Him and our gratefulness for eternal life.

JESUS IS NOT A SANTA CLAUS

Those who have never come into an intimate relationship with Jesus Christ mistakenly view Him as a sort of Santa Claus— Someone you turn to occasionally when you want something, Someone who loves to smile at people and never frowns or gets angry. A gift giver who only rewards and never punishes. This too is a groundless caricature of Jesus.

A caricature is a portrait of someone that greatly exaggerates certain features while minimizing others. Although caricatures are often funny, if people truly looked like their caricatures, they would be grotesque. Yes, the love we receive from God the Father and His Son are beyond anything we can describe or imagine. But His love is only one of His awesome attributes. God tells us that He is not solely a God of love. He also is a God of righteousness and justice. He delights in exercising these attributes just as He delights in exercising His love and kindness. But when we focus on only one of His attributes and turn a blind eye to the others, we embrace a caricature of God that distorts His character and nature, portraying Him very differently than He really is. God tells us that He wants us to *understand* what He is really like and to intimately know Him as He *really* is (see Jeremiah 9:23–24).

The Bible says God hates sin, evil, perversion, lies, greed, arrogance, and a host of other traits and activities. But fortunately for us, God is not only a God of righteousness and judgment; He also is a God of love and mercy. So much so in fact that He sacrificed His Son, expressing the whole of His wrath and judgment for our sins upon Christ—a sacrifice that fully atoned for all the sins of everyone who would place their faith in Jesus Christ and follow Him.

Jesus is in perfect unity with His Father—in love, in righteousness, and in judgment. Jesus loves everything and everyone His Father loves and hates everything His Father hates. While the Father sacrificed His Son for our sins, Jesus willingly sacrificed Himself and even interceded on our behalf in His prayer before His arrest (see John 17) and in His prayer from the cross, when He said, "Father, forgive them, for they do not know what they do" (Luke 23:34, NKJV). As you get to know Jesus intimately, you will discover that His love is infinitely greater than that of a mythical Santa. You'll also discover that His holiness, righteousness, and judgment make Him infinitely different.

So now that we know that Jesus did not come to earth to lead us into socialism or a new religion or to simply lavish us with gifts, the question we must answer is, why did He come to earth? What missions did He come to accomplish? The good news is we don't have to guess at the answer. Jesus already answered the question for us. As you'll see, He didn't come to accomplish just one mission; He came to accomplish twenty-seven that He identified. And, amazingly, He accomplished every one!

CHAPTER 16

WHY DID JESUS
COME TO EARTH?

*He was sent to accomplish
twenty-seven missions,
and He completed them all.*

That night two thousand years ago when a peasant girl named Mary gave birth to a baby boy was unlike any other night in human history. A bright star appeared over the stable where the baby lay in a manger. An angel appeared to a group of shepherds, momentarily terrifying them. The angel announced, "Do not be afraid. I bring you good news of great joy that will be for all the people. Today in the town of David a Savior has been born to you; he is Christ the Lord. This will be a sign to you: You will find a baby wrapped in cloths and lying in a manger" (Luke 2:10–12). Suddenly thousands of angels filled the sky, praising God and saying, "Glory to God in the highest, and on earth peace, goodwill toward men" (verse 14, NKJV).

A Savior? Christ the Lord? Who was this baby? Months

earlier an angel had appeared in a dream to Mary's husband, telling him he should name the baby Jesus, "for he shall save his people from their sins" (Matthew 1:21, KJV). The name *Jesus* literally means "Jehovah saves." And what did the angel mean by "Christ the Lord"? The word *Christ* was the Greek word for "anointed," which referred to Israel's long-awaited Messiah, whose coming had been foretold by the Jewish prophet Daniel six hundred years earlier.

When Jews in the first century heard the name *Jesus,* they heard "Jehovah saves," but why did people need to be saved from their sins? And why was a Messiah needed to save them? Through the Old Testament prophets, God had told Israel that a person's sin eternally separates him or her from God, who is holy and perfectly righteous. Every sinful thought, word, or deed by any man or woman, boy or girl, is a terrible offense against God. Every sin creates a debt.

Because we continue to sin even when we try not to, our sins mount up a debt so great that we could never pay off what we owe. Such a debt could only be paid by a perfect, sinless Being who could take upon Himself the full penalty for sin in place of the people who committed the sins. The only way peace could be restored between sinful humans and a holy God was for this debt to be satisfied and its penalty paid in full. And that is what the angels announced on the star-filled night of Jesus' birth. Amazingly, God had sent His only, perfectly righteous, holy Son to pay off the debt of sin for all who would believe in Him.

So, as foretold by God through His prophets and angels, Jesus had come to save God's people from the power and condemnation of sin. And while this was Jesus' primary mission, it wasn't His only mission. In His own words, Jesus identified twenty-seven missions that He came to accomplish. Amazingly, He completed every one of them! In addition to learning about His missions, we must understand His motivation or purposes for pursuing these missions. Purpose provides the power to endure adversity and overcome obstacles that could otherwise thwart a mission. And if our hope is to be followers of Jesus Christ, then His purposes will become our purposes. This is what will give us lasting motivation to follow His teachings and do what He instructs and leads us to do.

The Driving Purposes of Jesus' Life

Jesus stated three purposes that motivated virtually everything He did. There is also a fourth purpose that we can deduce from a number of His statements. His stated purposes center on His relationship with God the Father, while the fourth purpose centers on you and me. The overriding motives and purposes for everything Jesus did and said were to please the Father, honor the Father, and glorify the Father. Jesus said, "For I seek not to please myself but him who sent me" (John 5:30). "But I honor my Father and you dishonor me. I am not seeking glory for myself; but there is one who seeks it, and he is the judge" (John 8:49–50). In Jesus' prayer shortly before His arrest, He prayed, "I have brought you glory on earth by completing the work you gave me to do" (John 17:4).

Jesus also told us that He and the Father are one (see John 10:30), which means that Christ shares all the values, loves, and desires of the Father. Jesus told Nicodemus, "For God so loved the world that He gave His only begotten Son, that whoever believes in Him should not perish but have everlasting life" (John 3:16, NKJV). We can deduce that Jesus' actions, though motivated first and foremost by His love for the Father and His desire to please, honor, and glorify Him, are also motivated by an unimaginable love for us that He shares with the Father—a love so incomprehensible that it motivated the Father to sacrifice His only Son for us. In all, Jesus undertook twenty-seven missions, motivated by His love for the Father and His love for us.

THE EARTHLY MISSIONS OF JESUS

Throughout history men and women have embarked on missions that would determine the fate of their families, their communities, even their nations. Often the missions put lives at risk. If they succeeded, they would save their own lives and the lives of others. If they failed, people would die. In 1776, Benjamin Franklin embarked on one of the most important missions in American history. He had been commissioned by the Continental Congress to journey to France to plead for loans for America to wage its war of independence against Great Britain. If Franklin failed to acquire the loans, the war would be lost, and the democracy, along with its founders, would die. But as important as Franklin's mission was, it pales into insignificance when compared to the daunting missions Jesus undertook. No man in history has embarked on any mission in which the stakes were so high. If Jesus failed to accomplish His missions, every man, woman, boy, and girl who ever lived would be doomed—separated from God, with no hope of eternal life.

The missions Jesus revealed can be divided into two categories—primary or general missions and tactical or implementation missions. His primary missions permeated everything He said and did. They were His "why" missions—the true purposes and motives that drove His behavior and decision making. His tactical or implementation missions were the specific actions and activities He undertook to accomplish all that the Father had given Him to do. Whether a primary mission or a tactical mission, every one was critical. If He failed to achieve even one, God's work would be incomplete, and humanity would have forever remained spiritually dead.

Jesus' Primary or General Missions

1. To Testify About the Truth (John 18:37)

When confronted by Pontius Pilate, Jesus said, "For this cause I have come into the world, that I should bear witness to the truth" (John 18:37, NKJV). Why was this so critical? Simply stated, since sin had entered the world, humanity had been plagued by lies and illusions. God is as much a God of truth as He is a God of love—it is ingrained in His nature. And yet, for thousands of years humanity had believed lies and lived in illusion and darkness. People believed lies about God, His nature, and His values. They believed lies about themselves and lies perpetrated by the world, embracing the world's values instead of God's.

For example, the world values success and measures it by the amount of one's material wealth. But God measures success by the godliness of a person's heart, by a person's love for Him and others, and by the eternal fruit a person's life produces according to what he or she has been given. Jesus said, "What good will it be for a man if he gains the whole world, yet forfeits his soul?" and "A man's life does not consist in the abundance of his possessions" (Matthew 16:26; Luke 12:15). He also said, "You are the ones who justify yourselves in the eyes of men, but God knows your hearts. What is highly valued among men is detestable in God's sight" (Luke 16:15). Wow! We are so deceived by the illusions and lies of the world and its values that we often love what God hates and ignore or run away from what He loves. While *we* focus on the things we can *see,* God focuses on what can't be seen—our hearts and eternal values. To this end Jesus said, "Do not lay up for yourselves treasures on earth, where moth and rust destroy and where thieves break in and steal; but lay up for yourselves treasures in heaven, where neither moth nor rust destroys and where thieves do not break in and steal. For where your treasure is, there your heart will be also" (Matthew 6:19–21, NKJV).

This is why it was so critical that Jesus testified about the truth. Humanity is upside down, believing so many lies and illusions, so Jesus came to earth to set the record straight. Our only hope of stepping out of the illusion and lies was for Jesus to reveal the truth and the realities of this life and the truth about the life to come.

2. To Speak the Father's Words—Verbatim (John 12:49; 14:24; 17:14)

While Jesus was sent to earth to testify of the truth, He came with the understanding that the message would not be His own. Instead, He would teach *exactly* what His Father told Him to say. In John 12:49, Christ revealed to His disciples: "For I did not speak of my own accord, but the Father who sent me commanded me what to say and how to say it." In all, Jesus made more than nineteen hundred statements that were recorded by the New Testament writers. His statements were intended to become *the* central focus of every believer's life.

In Revelation 19, John tells us that an angel appeared before him, and John fell on his face to worship him. But the angel told him, "Do not do it" and explained that he was a fellow servant among those who have the "testimony of Jesus." He then told John, "Worship God! For the *testimony of Jesus* is the spirit of prophecy" (verse 10). In other words, the whole spirit or purpose of prophesy and all the revelations that John had been given was not just to reveal future events but rather to turn our hearts and minds back to the testimony of Jesus. This is not the testimony *about* Jesus but the testimony *of* Jesus—the life-giving statements that came out of His mouth. (Jesus made twenty amazing promises to you and me about His words that He didn't make about any other words. See appendix 2.)

3. To Be the Light of the World So His Followers Can Walk in Light (John 8:12; 9:5)

Jesus said, "I am the light of the world. Whoever follows me will never walk in darkness, but will have the light of life" (John 8:12). It wasn't enough for Jesus simply to testify of the truth—He also had to "turn the light on." He didn't settle for just telling us the truth; He proclaimed it in such a way that it could be clearly heard and understood. He had to provide such a bright light that it would open the eyes of those who were spiritually blind. And beyond proclaiming the truth, He demonstrated it. Jesus' life was the ultimate example of living the truth every moment. Jesus' words and life were a beacon of light that believers could follow as they journeyed through a spiritually dark world.

Living a life that was a moment-by-moment demonstration of perfect truth would be impossible for anyone else, but it wasn't difficult for Jesus because truth was His spiritual DNA. That's why He could honestly proclaim, "I am the way and the truth and the life" (John 14:6). His light was so bright that all who hungered for truth flocked to it. Unfortunately, according to Jesus, human nature loves darkness rather than light, because our deeds are evil (see John 3:19). Darkness is appealing because it provides the perfect habitat in which to nurture self-centeredness and our sinful nature.

This is why Jesus told Nicodemus that a person had to be born again in order to see and enter the kingdom of God. We need to receive a new nature that prefers to live in truth and light rather than illusion and darkness. "Everyone who does evil hates the light, and will not come into the light for fear that his deeds will be exposed. But whoever lives by the truth comes into the light, so that it may be seen plainly that what he has done has been done through God" (John 3:20–21). Once a person is born again, he or she not only has Jesus as the "light of life" to follow but also has a new nature that *desires* to walk in Christ's gloriously lit path. This is what makes it possible for a sinful human to see and do what Christ desires.

4. To Be the Bread of Life, Which Gives Life to All Who Partake of Him (John 6:48–50)

During the Israelites' forty years of wandering through the desert, God provided a daily supply of manna for every man, woman, and child. And though the bread kept them alive, they all eventually died. As wonderful as that miraculous bread was, Jesus claimed that He was an even better source of sustenance. He said, "I am the living bread which came down from heaven. If anyone eats of this bread, he will live forever; and the bread that I shall give is My flesh, which I shall give for the life of the world" (John

6:51, NKJV). Unlike the manna that came from heaven during the journey to the Promised Land, which only sustained one's life for a period of time, Jesus is the spiritual bread from heaven that provides *eternal* life. The bread that He offers is the sacrifice of His life for the life of the world. At the same time, the only people who will gain the eternal benefit of His sacrificed life are those who will eat of it. We know how to eat literal bread, but how can we eat of His flesh?

Through the apostle John, the Holy Spirit answered that question. Speaking of Jesus as the living Word of God, John said, "And the Word became flesh and dwelt among us, and we beheld His glory, the glory as of the only begotten of the Father, full of grace and truth" (John 1:14, NKJV). The "flesh" that Jesus left behind for us to eat was His recorded words. Jesus confirmed this in John 6:63: "It is the Spirit who gives life; the flesh profits nothing. The words that I speak to you are spirit, and they are life" (NKJV). We eat of His flesh by consuming His words—and His words produce spiritual life within us. He later said, "I tell you the truth, if anyone keeps my word, he will never see death" (John 8:51). So "eating" His words isn't just reading them; it is embracing His words by faith.

Beyond that, it involves obeying His words as we are empowered by His grace. When we truly believe in Him, our faith expresses itself by doing what His words tell us to do. And faith makes His words a part of our spiritual DNA, which produces life that continues for eternity. To this end Jesus said, "Heaven and earth will pass away, but my words will never pass away" (Matthew 24:35). And in Matthew 7:21–27, Jesus described saving faith as *hearing* what He said and *doing* it.

Not everyone who says to Me, "Lord, Lord," shall enter the kingdom of heaven, but he who does the will of My Father in heaven. Many will say to Me in that day, "Lord, Lord, have we not prophesied in Your name, cast out demons in Your name, and done many wonders in Your name?" And then I will declare to them, "I never knew you; depart from Me, you who practice lawlessness!"

Therefore whoever hears these sayings of Mine, and does them, I will liken him to a wise man who built his house on the rock: and the rain descended, the floods came, and the winds blew and beat on that house; and it did not fall, for it was founded on the rock. But everyone who hears these sayings of Mine, and does not do them, will be like a foolish man who built his house on the sand: and the rain descended, the floods came, and the winds blew and beat on that house; and it fell. And great was its fall. (NKJV)

While this passage may be troubling to many, it is as true as anything else Jesus said. This passage reveals that pseudofaith will collapse when a person comes face to face with Jesus Christ. But the faith of His true followers will withstand all the storms of life and the winds of judgment, because true faith is built on the rock of hearing His words and doing them. Does this mean that we earn eternal life through an all-out effort to be obedient? Absolutely not! Salvation results from being born again, and that birth comes solely by an act of God's grace. But the new birth produces saving faith, which expresses itself by a new desire to discover and do what Christ commands. By God's grace and the power of the indwelling Holy Spirit, we are able to do what He tells us. As we have seen, doing what He says becomes our way of loving Him (see John 14:21–23).

5. To Reveal the Father to Others (Matthew 11:27)

In Matthew 11:27, Jesus was speaking to His fellow Jews, who were people of the covenant and felt they knew all about the one true God. Yet Jesus told them that no one knew the Father intimately except the Son and those to whom the Son chose to reveal Him! (Whenever Jesus used the term *the Father,* He was referring to God the Father. Whenever He used the word *know,* He used the Greek word that in context refers to the type of knowing that encompasses intimacy.) So here He revealed that even though the Jews knew about God, they were not in an *intimate* relationship with God.

God announced six hundred years earlier through the prophet Jeremiah that the goal of a person's life—the purpose for living and a person's "glory"—should be to gain an understanding of who God really is and to intimately know Him (see Jeremiah 9:23–24, NKJV). Even though this is God's number-one desire for us, He is so different from us that the only way anyone could know Him intimately was for His Son and the Holy Spirit to reveal Him. Jesus later stated that eternal life is defined by this same kind of intimacy with God (see John 17:3).

6. To Make the Father Known (John 17:26)

By the time Jesus came to earth, Israel's religious leaders had blinded the eyes of an entire nation as to who God really was and what He desired from His people. They had replaced the truths of God with the doctrines and commandments of men. They not only blinded people's eyes to the realities of God, but they also created religious demands that crushed people under the weight of guilt and legalism. Jesus wanted the world to know the Father as He really is—all His attributes and values. He wanted the world to know that God delights in loving-kindness, mercy, and grace, as well as righteousness, truth, and justice. He revealed in John 17:26 that this mission included the work of making His Father known. He began this with twelve disciples. He needed to make the Father known to them so they, in turn, could make the Father known to the world.

To accomplish this, Jesus not only told them all they needed to know about the Father, but He literally showed them the Father through the words that He spoke and the life He lived. In John 14:9–11, Jesus told Philip and the rest of His disciples, "Don't you know me, Philip, even after I have been among you such a long time? Anyone who has seen me has seen the Father. How can you say, 'Show us the Father'? Don't you believe that I am in the Father, and that the Father is in me? The words I say to you are not just my own. Rather, it is the Father, living in me, who is doing his work. Believe me when I say that I am in the Father and the Father is in me; or at least believe on the evidence of the miracles themselves."

If you want to know what the Father is really like, discover everything Jesus said, and look at everything He did. In Jesus' words you will hear the Father expressing His heart, and in Jesus' behavior you'll see the Father living and working in and through Christ.

7. To Do His Father's Will (John 4:34; 6:38)

It was noon when Jesus and His disciples arrived at a town in Samaria. They had been walking since sunrise and were tired and hungry. His disciples went into the center of town to buy food while Jesus rested near a well. Before they came back, He engaged in conversation with a Samaritan woman. This was no ordinary conversation. Jesus used the encounter to reveal amazing truths about God and eternal life.

He confronted the woman about her godless life and admitted for the first time that He was the long-awaited Messiah. She ran back to her village to tell the men that she had found the Messiah. Shortly after she left, Jesus' disciples returned with food they had purchased and urged Jesus to eat. To their surprise He replied, "I have food to eat that you know nothing about." Puzzled, they said to one another, "Could someone have brought him food?" He then announced, "My food is to do the will of him who sent me and to finish his work" (see John 4:32–34).

The purpose of food is to provide the nourishment and energy our bodies need to survive and thrive. But Jesus revealed that the nourishment and energy He needed came from *doing* the will of God. When a person is hungry, it's hard to think about anything else. Yet Jesus was so passionate about doing His Father's will that it didn't zap His energy—it produced energy. And unlike an earthly meal that benefits one's body for only a few hours, doing the will of God produces benefits that last for eternity.

At the well in Samaria, Jesus' spiritual lunch resulted in the spiritual awakening of a God-defying woman. She was born again and immediately began witnessing to other Samaritans. The result was that a number of men came and heard Jesus teach. They became believers and convinced Jesus to remain in Samaria for two days to preach the gospel.

In John 6:38, Jesus reaffirmed that doing the Father's will was the reason He had come to earth. Why is it so important that we understand this? Because if we are to follow Christ, doing God's will in every circumstance and situation should become our spiritual food. It should be as much a part of our lives as eating. And often, doing His will is as easy as coming into the moment and recognizing the "white fields" that are right in front of us—those whom God brings into our paths on any given day. He doesn't require you to share your faith with everyone, but you are to be available to be or do whatever the Holy Spirit leads you to do in each moment.

8. To Do the Father's Work and Finish It (John 4:34; 9:4)

Creation was only the beginning of God's revealed work, and the creation of humanity was the crowning work of God's creation. But when Adam and Eve sinned, a whole new work of God began—namely the redemption of Adam's race. The nature of humanity had been forever changed, but God's nature never changes. He has always been the God of absolute truth, holy righteousness, and perfect justice. Adam and Eve lost their innocence before God, and their sin caused them to die spiritually. At that moment they lost their former intimacy with God. And because He is holy, He could not simply wave a magic wand and make everything better.

God's holiness required a payment for sin, and He revealed His plan for redeeming humanity immediately after Adam's fall. God told Satan, "I will put enmity between you and the woman, and between your offspring and hers; he [the Messiah] will crush your head, and you will strike his heel" (Genesis 3:15). From that moment God set His plan for redemption into motion. The dividing wall between Eve's offspring and Satan would be Jesus and His atoning sacrifice.

But before that could happen, God chose to call out a race of people that would receive and record His words. He inspired prophets to write much of the Old Testament to enable His people to discover who He was and what He valued. But that was just a beginning. Israel killed her prophets, forgot God's work and grace, and time after time chose to live in darkness rather than light. Jesus needed not only to do the Father's work of proclaiming and demonstrating the truths of the gospel but also to complete the work of God by providing the atonement for humanity's sin. Through His death and resurrection, Jesus provided the means of redemption and salvation for fallen humanity.

While Jesus could recruit others (including you and me) to join Him in doing the work of the Father, He alone could finish God's work on earth with His atoning death. From the cross, He proclaimed once and for all, "It is finished" (John 19:30). Not only had He completed the work of God's grace; He had paid the full debt of the sins of those who would believe on Him. In fact the Greek phrase that He uttered literally means "paid in full." That was the very phrase that was used to cancel debts when a debt was repaid in full.

9. To Become the Capstone of God's Work (Matthew 21:42)

A capstone is the final stone added to a building that completes the structure and gives it the strength to remain intact. In Matthew 21:42, Jesus said He was the fulfillment of Isaiah's prophesy: "The stone the builders rejected has become the capstone; the Lord has done this, and it is marvelous in our eyes." The rejection of Jesus by God's chosen people—and His crucifixion and resurrection—became the capstone of God's redeeming work. Though the people responsible for His execution meant it for evil, God meant it for good. His rejection by His people became the ultimate blessing to all humanity—people from every nation and race. Oh what a Savior! Oh what a God! And how wonderful that the first fifty thousand believers were Jews, from the same people who had rejected Him as their Messiah.

10. To Save the World from the Consequences and Condemnation of Sin (John 3:17)

Could there ever be a greater mission than to "save the world"? In the second chapter of Ephesians, Paul says that we all were dead in our sins, absolutely without hope. That was the condition of the entire human race when God sent Jesus to earth. Jesus said, "For God did not send His Son into the world to condemn the world, but that the world through Him might be saved" (John 3:17, NKJV). This was certainly the greatest of all Christ's missions, for if He failed to accomplish it, all of us would be forever doomed.

I have heard ministers use this verse to proclaim that Jesus' atonement saved every person who ever lived or ever will live on the earth. And yet, when read in its context, this verse exposes such talk as a misinterpretation. For in His statements immediately preceding and following it, Jesus said, "For God so loved the world that He gave His only begotten Son, that whoever believes in Him should not perish but have everlasting life. For God did not send His Son into the world to condemn the world, but that the world through Him might be saved. He who believes in Him is not condemned; but he who does not believe is condemned already, because he has not believed in the name of the only begotten Son of God" (John 3:16–18, NKJV).

The Greek word translated "world" is *kosmos,* which has multiple meanings. It can refer to the world, everyone in the world, or a large group of people. In the Greek, when a word has multiple meanings, the context determines which meaning applies. Since Jesus said that the criterion for being saved was believing in Him (in the context surrounding verse 17) and that those who didn't believe in Him were condemned, the word *kosmos* here refers to a large group of people who would come from populations throughout the world that would believe in Him. It does not refer to the whole of humanity.

11. To Create a Kingdom (John 18:37)

As we saw in chapter 15, Jesus did not come to earth to start a religion or to create a religious organization. His commission from God was infinitely greater than that. Following Jesus' arrest, Pontius Pilate asked Jesus, "Are You the King of the Jews?" To this, Jesus answered, "My kingdom is not of this world. If My kingdom were of this world, My servants would fight, so that I should not be delivered to the Jews; but now My kingdom is not from here." Pilate replied, "Are You a king then?" Jesus answered, "You say rightly that I am a king. For this cause I was born, and for this cause I have come into the world, that I should bear witness to the truth. Everyone who is of the truth hears My voice" (see John 18:33, 35–37, NKJV).

Pilate was taken aback by Jesus' response. Rather than denying that He was a king, Jesus affirmed that He was. In this one statement He told Pilate that He is a King and that He not only was born for a purpose but had come from another world into this world. And beyond that, He made it clear that He was born for the cause of revealing absolute truth. Pilate's answers were almost as amazing as Jesus' answers. He didn't think Jesus was crazy, nor did he think Jesus was lying. And, finally, he didn't think Jesus was guilty of anything. He told Jesus' accusers, "I find no fault in Him at all" (John 18:38, NKJV).

Jesus revealed that He is the King of a kingdom that is not "of this world." At first glance we would say He was speaking of a kingdom in heaven. While that is certainly true, a kingdom not of this world can just as easily mean a kingdom whose subjects are in the world but not of the world. In John 17:16, Jesus said of His disciples, "They are not of the world, just as I am not of the world" (NKJV). So His kingdom can refer to a kingdom of followers who have been born again (born from above) and are therefore no longer lovers of the world, and their citizenship is in a new heavenly kingdom even while they are living on earth. While Jesus did not come to earth to establish a religion or a religious organization, He did come to establish a kingdom.

In the following chapter, we will look at each of the miraculous "supporting" missions that Jesus came to earth to accomplish. Amazingly, He accomplished every one of them!

CHAPTER 17

JESUS' TACTICAL OR "IMPLEMENTATION" MISSIONS

*He accomplished sixteen
supporting missions to accomplish
His primary missions.*

In addition to the eleven primary missions that Jesus came to fulfill, He identified an additional sixteen missions and five assignments that He and God the Father agreed He must fulfill on earth. Entire books could be written about each of these missions, but my purpose here is simply to introduce each mission.

12. TO PERFECTLY FULFILL ALL OF GOD'S MORAL LAWS

In Matthew 5:17, Jesus said, "Do not think that I have come to abolish the Law or the Prophets; I have not come to abolish them but to fulfill them." Jesus' mission was twofold: to perfectly fulfill the letter of God's moral laws revealed in the Old Testament and to fulfill the spirit of God's laws that He revealed in the Sermon on the Mount (see Matthew 5–7). In leading a perfect life, Jesus had to avoid sinful attitudes, words, and actions as well as sinful thoughts, motives, and intentions. The slightest hint of any unrighteousness would have disqualified Him from being the perfect Lamb of God. He had to obey every command of His Father, every wish of His Father, and every prompting of the Holy Spirit. He had to respond perfectly to every situation and circumstance.

We are tempted to say, "Well, no big deal. After all, He was God!" The only problem was that He also was a man. Because He was "the seed of a woman," He possessed every weakness and frailty of the flesh and human nature. On the human side, He was like Adam—born free of any sin but capable of falling at any moment. Any failure to respond to His Father's will, even once, would have been sin. We are told that Jesus was tried and tempted in all points, just as we are, but without a single failing (see Hebrews 2:17–18). If He had failed, we all would be doomed to eternal separation from God. But He did not! Oh what a Savior!

13. TO GIVE HIS LIFE AS A RANSOM FOR MANY

For most of us, *ransom* means "payment." We think of movies in which a kidnapper calls a distraught parent and demands payment for the safe return of a child. Although a ransom is such a payment, it is more than that. A ransom represents one of the greatest injustices we can experience. Someone steals someone or something that belongs to us. We feel a sense of violation and loss that can't be understood by anyone who hasn't experienced it. The purpose of paying a ransom is to *buy back* what is already ours.

One of my closest friends spent millions of dollars building a business from a worthless start-up to a valuable, thriving company. Then the company was "stolen" through a hostile take-over—a takeover that was going to be disastrous for my friend, the other shareholders in the company, and the employees. The only way he could avert disaster was to sell everything he had, borrow every penny he could, and make financial commitments that would bankrupt him if he failed. He was forced to pay for a company he had already paid for. He was paying a ransom.

Nothing is more offensive than having to buy back what we have already paid for. And to add insult to injury, we are paying the ransom to a thief. That is exactly what Christ did in giving His life for us. That is a ransom.

Why a Ransom Was Necessary

God made the first humans in His image, without sin. But Adam and Eve together set God's command aside and turned their backs on Him. At that moment God's rightful possession, the crowning point of creation, sold themselves into sin. We have all followed in Adam and Eve's footsteps. Every day we wound the heart of our loving Father. But rather than turning His back on us, God chose to redeem us with the ultimate ransom. He paid the most costly, terrible ransom ever paid, to buy back what was rightfully His. The price was the life and blood of His Son.

God's Son became sin—the sin of every person ever born. To buy us back, He had to become the putrid, debasing thoughts and deeds of the most vile persons (see 2 Corinthians 5:21; 1 John 2:2). And on top of that, He had to experience an agonizing separation from His Father for the first time in eternity. He received all the Father's wrath and judgment against sin, not for anything He had done, but for everything we have done and will do. This is what Jesus was revealing when He said, "For even the Son of Man did not come to be served, but to serve, and to give his life as a ransom for many" (Mark 10:45).

14. TO BE EXECUTED ON A CROSS

From the beginning of Jesus' public ministry, He made it known that He came to earth to die. In His conversation with Nicodemus, Jesus said, "And as Moses lifted up the serpent in the wilderness, even so must the Son of Man be lifted up, that whoever believes in Him should not perish but have eternal life" (John 3:14–15, NKJV). Moses had attached a bronze snake to a pole, and all victims of poisonous snakebites who looked up to the bronze snake survived (see Numbers 21:8–9). Jesus told Nicodemus that He, like Moses' snake, would be lifted up on a pole.

The Romans had long used crucifixion as the most torturous form of capital punishment. To anyone who lived in Israel at the time of Christ, there would be only one conclusion to draw from Jesus' statement: He was going to be crucified. Later in His ministry Jesus said, "And I, if I am lifted up from the earth, will draw all peoples to Myself." John explained, "This He said, signifying by what death He would die" (John 12:32–33, NKJV).

Imagine living your life every day, from your earliest years, knowing that you were going to be crucified. Amazingly, Jesus knew this would be His lot before He came to earth. As we saw earlier, right after Adam sinned, God told Satan that He was going to put a dividing wall between Satan and humanity (see Genesis 3:15). God even gave His servant Abraham a taste of the anguish of this sacrifice when He told him to sacrifice *his* only son.

But unlike the case with Abraham and Isaac, when Christ was taken to the place of sacrifice, there would be no one to stay the executioner's hand.

When the time came for Jesus to present Himself as the perfect Sacrifice for our sins, He told His disciples, "Behold, we are going up to Jerusalem, and the Son of Man will be betrayed to the chief priests and to the scribes; and they will condemn Him to death, and deliver Him to the Gentiles to mock and to scourge and to crucify. And the third day He will rise again" (Matthew 20:18–19, NKJV).

In the minutes before delivering Christ's death sentence, Pontius Pilate said to Jesus, "'Do You not know that I have power to crucify You, and power to release You?'

"Jesus answered, 'You could have no power at all against Me unless it had been given you from above. Therefore the one who delivered Me to you has the greater sin'" (John 19:10–11, NKJV).

Even though Pilate thought it was his decision to sentence or pardon Christ, in reality it was Christ who was giving Himself up to atone for our sins. A few hours earlier, Jesus had told Peter, "Do you think I cannot call on my Father, and he will at once put at my disposal more than twelve legions of angels? But how then would the Scriptures be fulfilled that say it must happen in this way?" (Matthew 26:53–54). The Father and the Son had planned this before they created the world (see Matthew 25:34).

15. TO PREACH THE GOSPEL

Before Jesus sacrificed His life for us, He went throughout Judea for three and a half years, preaching the gospel. He couldn't sacrifice His life without first explaining why He would be giving up

His life. He needed to proclaim the gospel so that people would understand the context surrounding His atoning sacrifice. The call of His gospel needed to be clearly understood so that His work on the cross would bear all the fruit that He and the Father intended. In fact, Jesus began His public ministry by quoting Isaiah 61:1: "The Spirit of the LORD is upon Me, because He has anointed Me to preach the gospel to the poor" (Luke 4:18, NKJV; see also Mark 1:14–15, 38). The Greek word translated "gospel" means "glad tidings" or "good news." The Greek word translated "preach" means "to proclaim" or "announce publicly." Jesus proclaimed the good news of eternal life and the establishment of God's kingdom. He also revealed five specific assignments related to His mission of preaching the gospel. These assignments defined His focus and priorities as He proclaimed the good news.

Assignment 1: To Preach the Good News to the Poor

Jesus began the Sermon on the Mount with the statement "Blessed are the poor in spirit, for theirs is the kingdom of heaven" (Matthew 5:3; see also Luke 4:18). The Greek word He used for "poor" was *ptochos,* which refers to a "destitute, cowering beggar." Jesus proclaimed the good news of God's kingdom and eternal life to those who were spiritual beggars as well as those who were literal beggars. But His promise in the Sermon on the Mount was only to those who were "spiritual beggars," because they alone see their spiritual bankruptcy and are so desperate they turn to receive God's provision of eternal life. Jesus' first assignment in preaching the gospel was to boldly announce to all who see themselves as spiritually destitute that God stands ready to transfer His spiritual wealth and righteousness to their bankrupt accounts. None of us possesses the spiritual means to get into heaven. We can spend eternity in heaven only because God paid our debt.

Assignment 2: To Proclaim the Acceptable Year of the Lord

In this announcement, the word translated "year" doesn't mean a 365-day year. It means a period of time surrounding a specific event. Jesus was to publicly announce that a period of time had come in which humanity would be made "acceptable" to God (see Luke 4:19, NKJV). That period of time began with Jesus' coming to earth. It will end when He returns to earth in His second coming. For a period of time surrounding the event of Christ's redemptive work, God Himself would miraculously make us acceptable in spite of our sin.

Assignment 3: To Preach the Good News of God's Kingdom

Have you ever been locked out of your house or car? I have, too many times to count. It seems that I'm never locked out when time is not an issue. No, I find myself locked out when I'm in a hurry. I desperately need to gain entrance, but I am helpless to unlock the door. Throughout His ministry, Jesus told parables that revealed different aspects of God's kingdom. The one thing that seems to appear in each parable is that the entrance to God's kingdom is securely locked, and the only way to gain entrance is to enter through the door or gate that God must open (see Matthew 7:13–14; John 10:7; John 14:6).

In Luke 4:43, Jesus told His disciples, "I must preach the kingdom of God to the other cities also, because for this purpose I have been sent" (NKJV). He would proclaim the kingdom of God throughout the region. God's kingdom had come to earth, and although its door had been shut and locked, it was now being opened through the atoning sacrifice of God's Son. We can enter God's kingdom through our faith in the Lord Jesus Christ! Think of the relief and joy you feel when the door of your car or house is finally unlocked. If such a small event brings relief and joy, how much greater should our joy be when we realize that God has unlocked the door to His kingdom and ushered us in?

Assignment 4: To Proclaim Freedom for the Prisoners

Many years ago one of my friends whose net worth was more than $100 million was sentenced to prison for a violation of the Securities and Exchange Commission (SEC) laws. After his release he told me that even though he had been in a white-collar-crimes prison, it was still devastating. He had lost the freedom that he'd always taken for granted. In prison everything was determined by someone else. Of course, the freedom he missed the most was the opportunity to spend time with his wife and children. And he could do nothing to reclaim that freedom, aside from serving out his sentence.

The Bible teaches us that even though we think we are free, we are all prisoners of a terrible taskmaster—namely, sin. And like my friend, we have no power to free ourselves, no matter how badly we want to be set free. Then we hear Jesus say He has come to proclaim our freedom—from sin and its terrible consequence of eternal separation from God. He is opening the prison door that no one else can open (see Luke 4:18). One of my favorite songs is the Gaither Vocal Band rendition of "Let Freedom Ring," which says, "Let freedom echo through the lonely streets where prisons have no key; you can be free and you can sing 'let freedom ring'!"[15]

Oh what a Savior, who would sacrifice His life so that He could open our prison doors!

Assignment 5: To Call Sinners to Repentance

Have you ever wondered if you could become less self-centered and more like Christ? David cried out, "My sin is ever before me" (Psalm 51:3, NASB). The apostle Paul exclaimed, "O wretched man that I am! Who will deliver me from this body of death?" (Romans 7:24, NKJV). And Paul described us as "dead" in sin and in the world, having no hope (see Ephesians 2:1, 12). Without a doubt, one of the greatest announcements I have heard is the one found in Luke 5:32, when Jesus told the Pharisees, "I have not come to call the righteous, but sinners, to repentance" (NKJV). Jesus not only showed us the path to heaven; He also called on us to make a U-turn to get there through repentance. And by His grace, He gave us the faith and power to make that turn.

16. TO SEEK AND SAVE THE LOST

This is the sixteenth mission that Jesus mentioned. The nineteenth chapter of Luke records the born-again experience of a deeply hated sinner and his family. As we saw earlier, Zacchaeus had become wealthy at the expense of Jericho's hardworking citizens. As a chief tax collector, he had cheated many of them by collecting more taxes than they owed. But after hearing Jesus, he and his family were born again.

After Jesus had acknowledged the salvation of Zacchaeus and his family, Jesus made a statement that revealed a mission that went hand in hand with His mission of calling sinners to repentance. He said, "For the Son of Man came to seek and to save what was lost" (Luke 19:10). So Jesus didn't come to earth only to call sinners to repentance; He also came to actively pursue and seek out those of us who were hopelessly lost. And as if that were not enough, once the sinners were found, His mission was to save them! Fortunately for you and me, we were among the sinners He sought out and saved. Not only did He apply His righteousness to our debt, but He also empowered us with His grace to believe in Him and to gain the desire and power to repent of our sin.

17. TO LAY DOWN HIS LIFE FOR HIS SHEEP

In the tenth chapter of the gospel of John, Jesus compares His followers to sheep and Himself to the shepherd. In verse 11 He says, "I am the good shepherd. The good shepherd gives His life for the sheep" (NKJV). And in verse 15 He says, "And I lay down My life for the sheep" (NKJV). What's the difference between giving His life for the sheep and laying down His life for the sheep? The giving of His life included everything He did during His life on earth—His nurturing of us, His teaching us, and His leading us by living a life that was the perfect example of how God wants us to live. And as if that weren't enough, He then chose to lay down His life to save His sheep from the deadly consequences of their sin. He replaced the judgment that awaited us with a promise of judgment-free eternal life.

18. TO GIVE HIS SHEEP ETERNAL LIFE

After telling us He is the Good Shepherd, Jesus defined exactly who His sheep are and revealed yet another of His missions. He said, "My sheep hear My voice, and I know them, and they follow Me. And I give them eternal life, and they shall never perish; neither shall anyone snatch them out of My hand" (John 10:27–28, NKJV). In Jesus' day, sheep of different flocks often grazed hillsides together and were even penned together. When it was time for a shepherd to separate his sheep from the flocks of other shepherds, he would call his sheep with a loud call or song that was his unique call. Each flock recognized their shepherd's voice and call and would come out from among the other flocks. In John 10:27, Jesus tells us that His sheep aren't just any sheep; they are a specific flock. His sheep hear His voice and His call, and they follow Him. They are people who follow His example, follow His teachings, and follow the path He walks.

After Jesus defined who His sheep are, He revealed His mission in verse 28. He gives His sheep eternal life; they will never die, and no one will ever snatch them out of His hand. But He does more than give them eternal life; He will forever lead them, and no one in heaven, on earth, or under the earth will steal them away. He also protects them from the onslaught of any enemy they may encounter. And to do all this, He not only had to purchase their salvation with His death; He had to raise Himself from the grave. (A dead shepherd cannot protect His sheep.) That's why Jesus said in John 10:17–18, "The reason my Father loves me is that I lay down my life—only to take it up again. No one takes it from me, but I lay it down of my own accord. I have authority to lay it down and authority to take it up again. This command I received from my Father." What other shepherd would die for us and then raise Himself from the dead to give us eternal life and eternal protection? Oh what a Shepherd!

19. TO GIVE ABUNDANT LIFE TO HIS SHEEP

Before Jesus came to earth, others had claimed to be the Messiah. They urged their fellow Jews to follow their leading. But none came with the teachings, the authority, the power, or the miracles that were present in the ministry of Jesus. In John 10:10, Jesus distinguished Himself from the others, calling them thieves. He said, "The thief does not come except to steal, and to kill, and to destroy. I have come that they [His sheep] may have life, and that they may have it more abundantly" (NKJV). Jesus didn't come just to save the lives of the sheep. His mission was also to give them a more abundant life. The Greek word translated "abundantly" is *perissos,* which means "exceedingly full beyond measure" or "filled to the point that it can't be contained" or "gushing and overflowing." We could paraphrase this statement to read: "I have come that My sheep might have life and that they might have life that is so full it can't be measured and in fact is gushing and overflowing to the point that it can't be contained." This is in perfect keeping with His promise in John 7:38, when Jesus said that those who truly believe in Him will have rivers of Living Water flowing out of their innermost being.

The mission Jesus revealed in John 10:10 is providing, not wealth or an abundance of material possessions, but rather an abundance of life! In fact, Jesus warned, "Watch out! Be on your guard against all kinds of greed; a man's life does not consist in the abundance of his possessions" (Luke 12:15). So how does Jesus define an abundance of life? In Jeremiah 9:24, God tells us we are to glory in our intimacy with Him. And in John 17:3, Jesus defines eternal life itself as intimately knowing the Father and the Son.

Out of that intimacy flows an abundance of life that fills our deepest needs and longings and overflows to bless those whom God brings into our paths. Out of our intimacy with the Father, the Son, and the Holy Spirit flow unquenchable joy, inexplicable peace, immeasurable strength, miraculous ministry, and a never-ending source of God's love and grace to us and through us to others.

20. TO LOSE NONE OF THOSE WHO WERE GIVEN TO HIM

In the sixth chapter of John, Jesus told a group of nonbelievers that everyone the Father gives to Him will come to Him in faith. And whoever comes to Him, He will not reject. Then He said, "And this is the will of him who sent me, that I shall lose none of all that he has given me, but raise them up at the last day" (verse 39). Imagine a shepherd with millions of sheep on mountains all over the world. How many sheep would get lost? How many would be killed or eaten by other animals? How impossible would it be for one shepherd to protect and care for all the sheep without losing one? And yet that describes this mission the Father gave Jesus to accomplish.

Jesus fulfilled this mission: to protect and care for every sheep the Father had given Him; He provided eternal life to them and raised them from the dead. He fulfilled it to the letter while He was on earth and continues to fulfill it today. One point that must not be missed is Jesus' love and attention to each of us as individuals. His attention and care are focused on each one of us—He knows us intimately and loves us and calls us by name to follow Him through life on earth.

21. TO FORGIVE SINS

When Jesus entered Capernaum, He went into a large house and began to preach. The house was so crowded that four men carrying a man who was paralyzed could not get near its entrance. After climbing onto the roof, they hoisted up their paralyzed friend. Then, breaking through the roof itself, they lowered the man to the floor in front of Jesus. "When Jesus saw their faith, he said to the paralytic, 'Son, your sins are forgiven'" (Mark 2:5). Some of the religious leaders in the room began to think, "Why does this fellow talk like that? He's blaspheming! Who can forgive sins but God alone?" (verse 7). Then Jesus challenged them: "Why do you reason about these things in your hearts? Which is easier, to say to the paralytic, 'Your sins are forgiven you,' or to say, 'Arise, take up your bed and walk'?" (verses 8–9, NKJV). The answer is both are impossible for humans. Only God can do either.

Then Jesus made a statement that no other person in history could have authoritatively made. He said, "But that you may know that the Son of Man has authority on earth to forgive sins..." (verse 10). He turned to the paralytic and said, "I say to you, arise, take up your bed, and go to your house" (verse 11, NKJV). The paralytic was immediately healed, and everyone present was amazed and glorified God, saying, "We have never seen anything like this!" (verse 12). More amazing than the miracle of the paralytic's healing was the fact that a man had the authority to forgive sins. Only God could forgive sin, and in a single moment Jesus had announced and proved that He was God. Not only did He have the authority and power to forgive, but He had been commissioned by the Father to do just that. He fulfilled this mission, even as He was dying on the cross. He died for us, paying off our incalculable debt, and He forgave us as well. And lest the Father execute His wrath against the ones who executed and mocked His Son, Jesus even petitioned the Father to forgive them (see Luke 23:34). Is there anyone like Him? Not one!

22. To Serve

In Matthew 20, we see Jesus teaching His disciples on the subject of leadership. With one short teaching, He revealed the principle of leadership in God's kingdom. If would-be leaders would live out this principle, they could fail at all the other principles and still be great leaders. Jesus told them, "You know that the rulers of the Gentiles lord it over them, and those who are great exercise authority over them. Yet it shall not be so among you; but whoever desires to become great among you, let him be your servant. And whoever desires to be first among you, let him be your slave—just as the Son of Man did not come to be served, but to serve, and to give His life a ransom for many" (verses 25–28, NKJV). An effective leader is a servant. Jesus said, "The Son of Man did not come to be served, but to serve."

He came to earth to serve His Father. Jesus lived in perfect obedience to the Father's will. But Jesus' serving didn't end with serving the Father. He served all those He led as well, to the point of washing their feet on the night of His arrest. And last but not least, He served us, giving His life for us. And yet even with His death, He didn't stop serving us. To this very moment, He continues to shepherd us and lead us to places of safety and blessing. He serves and leads us through the ministry of the Holy Spirit. As our "high priest" (see Hebrews 4:14), He intercedes for us before the

Father. Oh that we might gain His servant's heart—and embrace His mission to become the servants of all!

23. TO RELEASE THE OPPRESSED

At the time Jesus came to earth, Israel had been under Roman rule and oppression for nearly sixty years. The Jews were hoping the Messiah would come and supernaturally deliver them from their oppressors. When Jesus announced that He had come to "release the oppressed," surely their hope for deliverance from Rome was kindled (see Luke 4:18). But Jews and gentiles alike were living under a far greater oppression than that of Rome—an oppression that couldn't be ended by an army or an armistice. The greatest oppression that men and women can ever experience is enslavement to sin. Sin's sure consequence is death and eternal separation from God. And yet, in His death and resurrection, Jesus provided the ultimate release from the ultimate oppressor. He sets free all who follow Him by faith, to walk in the newness of life to serve in His all-volunteer army. An army, not of oppressors, but of deliverers—living and proclaiming the gospel of God's kingdom to a desperate world.

24. TO HEAL THE BLIND

Jesus, quoting Isaiah, announced His ministry and a number of His missions. Part of this mission was to "proclaim liberty to the captives and recovery of sight to the blind" (Luke 4:18, NKJV). Jesus talked of two types of blindness—physical and spiritual—and offered healing for both. We have read the stories of the blind men He healed. And to His disciples He said, "Do you still not see or understand? Are your hearts hardened? Do you have eyes but fail to see, and ears but fail to hear?" (Mark 8:17–18). Ultimately, He healed their spiritually hardened hearts, blind eyes, and deaf ears. And the gospel writers made references that indicate Jesus healed many more who were blind, perhaps hundreds or even thousands. The apostle John closed his gospel with this statement: "Jesus did many other things as well. If every one of them were written down, I suppose that even the whole world would not have room for the books that would be written" (John 21:25). However, as many as He physically healed, He has healed the spiritual blindness of millions more. People cannot see themselves as they really are, nor see Christ as He really is, unless their spiritually blind eyes are healed (see Revelation 3:18–20).

25. To Sanctify Himself and Those Who Would Follow Him

In His final prayer before His arrest, Jesus said, "For them I sanctify myself, that they too may be truly sanctified" (John 17:19). As we saw in an earlier chapter, the word *sanctify* comes from the Greek word *hagiazo,* which is derived from the root word *hagios.* This word means "to set apart" or living in the state of having been set apart. However, when used in Scripture, *hagiazo* implies a state of being separated from sin and the values of the world, being set apart to God for His use and purposes, and living in righteousness. Jesus kept Himself set apart to God, not only because of His nature and His love for the Father, but in order to be an example to us as well. In verse 17, Jesus said, "Sanctify them by the truth; your word is truth." God uses His Word and its truth to set us apart to Him and for His use. Shortly before His prayer, Jesus told His disciples, "You are already clean because of the word I have spoken to you" (John 15:3). We see Jesus accomplishing this mission in our lives by using His Word not only to sanctify us but also to cleanse and purify us.

26. TO RAISE HIMSELF FROM THE DEAD

In John 10:17–18, Jesus revealed that another of His missions was to raise Himself from the dead. He said, "I lay down my life—only to take it up again. No one takes it from me, but I lay it down of my own accord. I have authority to lay it down and authority to take it up again. This command I received from my Father." Our temptation is to think, *This is no big deal. After all, He's God.* But this was a very big deal, because Jesus said that laying down His life and taking it up again was one of the reasons His Father loved Him in such a special way. Although we never will have more than a superficial understanding of the degree of suffering Jesus experienced, at least we can understand the nature of His suffering.

But how can we begin to understand what He had to do to raise Himself from the dead? He had to demonstrate a level of faith we can't even begin to imagine. Perhaps it was His tremendous obedience and faith that so affected the Father's love for His Son. But in spite of our inability to comprehend this act of obedience and faith, it is nonetheless an impossible mission, perfectly executed by the God-Man, Jesus. And by raising Himself, He proved that He has the power and authority to raise us up as well.

27. To Bring a Fire to Earth That Divides the Righteous from the Unrighteous

This last revealed mission of Jesus on earth is the least understood and the least talked about. It's also one of the most surprising. He said, "I have come to bring fire on the earth, and how I wish it were already kindled! But I have a baptism to undergo, and how distressed I am until it is completed! Do you think I came to bring peace on earth? No, I tell you, but division. From now on there will be five in one family divided against each other, three against two and two against three. They will be divided, father against son and son against father, mother against daughter and daughter against mother, mother-in-law against daughter-in-law and daughter-in-law against mother-in-law" (Luke 12:49–53).

Jesus is not Gandhi. Nor is He the pope or the head of any church denomination. Gandhi, the pope, and leaders of various denominations are humans. They are often inclined to do everything they can to promote and maintain peace—even if truth or righteousness is compromised. Not so with Jesus. He knew that He and His message would not be the unifying, peacemaking factor for all humanity. To the contrary. Jesus divided people into two categories—those who love darkness rather than light and those who love and follow the truth. And since He claimed to be the way, the truth, and the life, He knew that He would be the dividing line between those who would embrace God and those who would continue to be their own god. It doesn't matter if that line runs between two nations or through a family.

Those who want to be the god of their own lives will never be in unity with those who choose to deny themselves, take up their crosses, and follow Jesus. Is He saying that His followers should shun nonbelievers? Absolutely not! We are to follow His example and take the gospel to every creature—both in what we say and how we live. What He is saying is that because people naturally love darkness rather than light, unless they are born again, they will not want to be close to those who love truth and light and choose to follow Christ.

From the first century until now, many who have chosen to follow Jesus have been ostracized, abandoned, and disowned by their families. Millions have been persecuted or martyred because they chose to follow Christ. But as the apostle Paul taught in 2 Corinthians 4:17–18, this "momentary, light affliction is producing for us an eternal weight of glory far beyond all comparison" (NASB). Today, even in America, Christians are demeaned, ridiculed, and called bigots because they adhere to biblical teachings regarding marriage and family relationships, the sanctity of life, and the sinfulness of adultery and homosexuality. As followers of Christ, we must walk the same line He walked—actively loving and pursing nonbelievers and yet holding firm to the truths that define the difference between the darkness of sin and the righteousness of God.

Jesus completed twenty-seven impossible missions while He was on earth. But His work did not end with His ascension into heaven. He revealed six additional missions that He would accomplish after He returned to the Father, and those will be our focus in the next chapter.

CHAPTER 18

P.S.: Jesus Isn't Done Yet

Here are the six missions Jesus began after He ascended to heaven.

We have discussed the twenty-seven missions that Jesus accomplished during His brief life on earth. But we know that He continues to be active in the lives of His followers. Jesus revealed at least six missions that He would perform after He returned to His Father—missions that are critically important to our lives and accomplishing the missions He set before us. Here are Jesus' six post-ascension missions.

1. To Ask the Father to Send the Holy Spirit

In His upper-room conversation with His disciples, Jesus said, "I will not leave you as orphans" (John 14:18) and promised to ask the Father to send the Holy Spirit. He revealed ten ministries that the Holy Spirit would perform on earth. Jesus had already said the first ministry of the Holy Spirit would be to give a second birth to one's spirit (see John 3:5–8). The other ministries of the Spirit are as follows:

1. Teach us all things and guide us into all truth (see John 14:26; 16:13)

2. Cause us to remember everything Jesus said to us (see John 14:26)

3. Be a testifying witness of Christ to us and through us (see John 15:26–27)

4. Be our Helper, Comforter, and Counselor (see John 16:7)

5. Convict nonbelievers of their sin (see John 16:8–9)

6. Reveal the righteousness of Christ (see John 16:10)

7. Reveal the condemning judgment of God (see John 16:11)

8. Reveal future events to believers (see John 16:13)

9. Indwell believers to provide them with spiritual power (see John 14:17; Acts 1:8)

10. Enable believers to be powerful witnesses of Christ (see Acts 1:8)

Jesus has fulfilled His mission of asking the Father to send the Holy Spirit. The Spirit was sent, and ever since the Day of Pentecost, believers and the world at large have not been the same.

2. TO ANSWER PRAYERS AND PETITIONS REQUESTED IN HIS NAME

In His upper-room conversation with His disciples, Jesus revealed yet another mission that He would accomplish after His ascension. In John 14:13–14, He said, "And I will do whatever you ask in my name, so that the Son may bring glory to the Father. You may ask me for anything in my name, and I will do it." Theologians have debated whether this promise was made only to the eleven disciples or if it was a general promise to all believers throughout history. I have seen countless miracles take place, including my son being healed of cancer and a dear friend's brother being healed of leukemia, after men and women of God have asked in Jesus' name. While this promise was certainly intended for the apostles, I have to believe it also is intended for all true followers of Christ.

One question should be seriously considered. What does Jesus mean by the phrase "in my name"? It does not mean simply ending a prayer with the words "In Jesus' name, amen." We end our prayers in His name because His atonement is the reason we have the opportunity to come directly to the Father. However, asking for something "in Jesus' name" is an entirely different matter. Under Roman law, an ambassador or a military attaché could issue a proclamation or an order "in the name of Caesar." However, he could only say that if he had a written authorization from Caesar that spelled out exactly what he could say—to the smallest detail—in Caesar's name. If he varied from the written authorization in the slightest, he could be executed. In fact, if he represented anything in the name of Caesar without Caesar's authorization, he could be executed. So speaking "in the name of Caesar" meant saying precisely what Caesar would say if he were present.

I believe that to ask for something "in Jesus' name," a believer should have an inner assurance that if Jesus were present, He would ask for that specific thing or outcome. Acting and praying in His name carries with it a tremendous responsibility. There are occasions when I have the confidence of knowing that if Jesus were present, He would ask for the thing I would ask for. For example, I believe that Jesus wanted my book *The Greatest Words Ever Spoken* to be translated into Spanish and Romanian. So I had no problem asking for that to be done "in His name." However, there have been times I have wanted something desperately and felt that receiving it could fall within His will, but I did *not* have either the peace or the faith to ask for it in His name. Some of those times other believers asked for that very thing to be done "in the name of Jesus Christ," and it was done. They (unlike me) had a perfect peace about asking in His name. God granted them the faith, and He honored their faith's expression.

3. TO PREPARE A PLACE IN HEAVEN
FOR HIS FOLLOWERS

In John 14:2–3, Jesus told His worried disciples, "In My Father's house are many mansions; if it were not so, I would have told you. I go to prepare a place for you. And if I go and prepare a place for you, I will come again and receive you to Myself; that where I am, there you may be also" (NKJV). Jesus revealed this mission and assured us by His promise that He would not abandon us to death but would come back and take us to be with Him. This is not meant just for His original disciples. The Second Coming of Christ is talked about throughout the writings of the apostles. And concerning His kingdom in heaven, Paul wrote, "Eye hath not seen, nor ear heard, neither have entered into the heart of man, the things which God hath prepared for them that love him" (1 Corinthians 2:9, KJV). Although we have no idea what "prepare a place for you" really entails, we know that what Jesus is preparing will be far more wonderful than we can imagine.

4. To Return to Earth and Take Us to Be with Him

The second half of Jesus' promise in John 14:3 revealed what has become one of His most talked-about and anticipated missions—namely, His Second Coming. He said, "And if I go and prepare a place for you, I will come again, and receive you to Myself; that where I am, there you may be also" (NASB). While His Second Coming will be the second most glorious event in history, I do not believe that He intended it to become the *dominant* focus of Christians. His words about His Second Coming were few and were intended to provide comfort, hope, and a powerful motivation to follow Him with diligence and a sense of urgency. In fact, the angel who appeared to the apostle John stated, "For the testimony of Jesus is the spirit of prophecy" (Revelation 19:10). Prophesy was given to us so that terrifying events wouldn't take us by surprise and deter our following Christ. But the purpose behind that purpose, or the spirit of prophesy, is the testimony of Jesus. In other words, prophecy is to point our eyes and ears back to the words of the Savior, to focus our faith and efforts on doing all that He instructs and commands. Notice that the angel in Revelation didn't say the testimony *about* Jesus was the spirit of prophesy but rather the testimony *of* Jesus—those awesome words that flowed out of His heart into the ears of His disciples and were recorded for us!

5. To Raise Up on the Last Day Those Who Were Given to Him

Can you imagine millions of saints who died throughout the ages, now in glorified bodies, rising from their graves, their ashes, and their resting places in the seas? According to Christ's statement in John 6:39–40, this is exactly what will happen—and very possibly in the not-too-distant future. Jesus said, "And this is the will of him who sent me, that I shall lose none of all that he has given me, but raise them up at the last day. For my Father's will is that everyone who looks to the Son and believes in him shall have eternal life, and I will raise him up at the last day."

6. TO JUDGE HUMANITY

This is the one mission of Jesus that no one can joyfully look forward to. Think what a tragedy it would be to have missed the purpose of life—that of loving and serving the one true God. To discover all that He did to make it possible for you to enjoy an intimate relationship with Him, only to realize you ignored all His whispers. How sad to have exchanged everything that has eternal worth for that which lasted only a short lifetime. To discover that God sacrificed His one and only Son to offer you eternal life, only to realize you trampled over His unimaginable sacrifice. And as if that's not bad enough, to have to go through God's judgment—revisiting all your thoughts, words, and deeds that were so offensive to Him. And then to bear an eternal sentence for all you did and said, when it could have been avoided. And yet, this is exactly what awaits those who haven't followed Christ (see Matthew 12:36–37).

Jesus said, "Moreover, the Father judges no one, but has entrusted all judgment to the Son" (John 5:22). The good news is that those who have truly believed in Jesus and have followed Him will not go through this judgment. According to the apostle

Paul, Christians will pass before the "judgment seat of Christ" (2 Corinthians 5:10), but the word translated as "judgment" is very different from the word used in relation to nonbelievers. The Greek word used for the "judgment seat" is *bema,* which means a "rewards seat." It was a word that was used to describe the seat at games from which a Greek or Roman official would hand out rewards to the winners of an event. No losers ever appeared before the bema seat.

On the other hand, the word used in John 5:22 and other places where the Lord talks about the judgment is the Greek word *krisis.* This word denotes a "trial," a "condemnation," or a "condemning sentence." And when it comes to the judgment of nonbelievers, Jesus also said, "As for the person who hears my words but does not keep them, I do not judge him. For I did not come to judge the world, but to save it. There is a judge for the one who rejects me and does not accept my words; that very word which I spoke will condemn him at the last day. For I did not speak of my own accord, but the Father who sent me commanded me what to say and how to say it" (John 12:47–49). The standards to be used in judging nonbelievers are the words that Jesus spoke. This is the judgment to which "professing believers," who were not truly born again, will also be subject.

Why do true believers in Christ not go through the condemning judgment that Jesus talked about? The answer is that Christ has already been judged, condemned, and executed in their place. The full punishment of their sin has been carried out—the full payment for their sin has already been made. Oh what a Savior!

My dear reader, if you have accepted in your mind that Jesus is the Christ, but you have not taken His words to heart and have not become His follower in word and deed, I urge you to prayerfully reread chapters 5 through 7 and fully surrender your life to our glorious, risen Savior. May God bless you beyond your wildest imagination in your pursuit of God and in your relationship of love and intimacy with the Father, the Son, and the Holy Spirit.

CHAPTER 19

THE LAST CHAPTER
IS *YOURS* TO WRITE

Jesus completed His missions without fail. How will you respond to the missions He has given you?

After telling Nicodemus that the only way to enter the kingdom of God was to be "born again," Jesus said, "This is the verdict: Light has come into the world, but men loved darkness instead of light because their deeds were evil. Everyone who does evil hates the light, and will not come into the light for fear that his deeds will be exposed. But whoever lives by the truth comes into the light, so that it may be seen plainly that what he has done has been done through God" (John 3:19–21).

To Pontius Pilate, Jesus said, "For this cause I was born, and for this cause I have come into the world, that I should bear witness to the truth. Everyone who is of the truth hears My voice" (John 18:37, NKJV). And He said to the religious leaders of His day, "And if I tell the truth, why do you not believe Me? He who is of God hears God's words; therefore you do not hear, because you are not of God" (John 8:46–47, NKJV). Finally, to all who would follow Him, Jesus said, "I am the light of the world. He who follows Me shall not walk in darkness, but have the light of life" (John 8:12, NKJV).

Jesus says that men and women will either run to the truth and the light or they will run away from it. He says that His followers will choose not to remain in darkness but instead will walk in the light and that He will always provide light and truth. He sums it all up by saying, "I am the way and the truth and the life. No one comes to the Father except through me" (John 14:6).

What has Jesus been saying to you? Where do you stand? Where do you want to go? Are you experiencing a growing hunger to discover His Word? Do you have a growing desire for a more intimate daily experience with the God who describes Himself as a God of "lovingkindness, judgment, and righteousness" (Jeremiah 9:24, NKJV)? Do you desire to run into the light or run away from it?

As you have seen, Jesus issued a call to follow Him, not to pray a prayer to accept or receive Him. He said, "If anyone would come after me, he must deny himself and take up his cross and follow me" (Matthew 16:24). He said, "My sheep hear My voice, and I know them, and they follow Me" (John 10:27, NKJV). Being a Christian isn't defined by the opinions or doctrines we embrace in our minds but rather by the beliefs in our hearts—beliefs that result in a turning away from self-centeredness to a total surrender of our lives to the lordship of Jesus Christ. Christians are born again, resulting in new beliefs in their hearts that produce a driving desire to follow Jesus Christ by discovering and doing what

He says to do. Christians make His words the guiding light of their beliefs, actions, decisions, and choices (see Matthew 7:24–25). All of this flows freely from the grace of God and is embraced and experienced by faith.

To all who want to follow Him, Jesus said, "As the Father has sent Me, I also send you" (John 20:21, NKJV). The Father did not send Jesus to earth to do whatever He wanted. He sent Him with specific missions and mission assignments. And just as the Father sent Jesus, He now sends us with specific missions, activities, and actions that we are to pursue throughout our lives. And because we have only a limited amount of time, Jesus calls us to be diligent in our pursuit of these missions.

James wrote, "What is your life? You are a mist that appears for a little while and then vanishes" (James 4:14). The apostle Paul wrote, "See then that you walk circumspectly, not as fools but as wise, redeeming the time, because the days are evil. Therefore do not be unwise, but understand what the will of the Lord is" (Ephesians 5:15–17, NKJV). Jesus reveals God's will for the direction of your life. He also, through His teachings, promises, and commands, reveal's God's perfect will for every issue, circumstance, and decision you face. And through the ministry of the Holy Spirit, you have free access to God's power to help you do everything Christ calls you to do.

God loves you so much that He gave His only begotten Son to die for you. But His love didn't stop at the Cross. He invites you to a life of intimacy with Him every moment of every day.

The last two pages of this chapter are for you to use for writing out your thoughts concerning Jesus Christ and your desire to follow Him. Take this opportunity to write down your thoughts in general and then to lay out a detailed set of ideas or plans for getting to know Him better. Listen to the Holy Spirit, and write out what He is saying to you.

For help in your walk with the Lord, check out Greatest words.com. You'll find helpful material, much of which is free. I know that God desires to bless you beyond anything you can imagine.

God Gives the Second Birth to a Samaritan

*To others, they were worse
than a dog. To Jesus, they were
a white field ready for harvest!*

To the Jews of Jesus' day, gentiles were considered to be on par with stray dogs. And Samaritans were considered to be even lower than gentiles. Observant Jews avoided all contact with them, considering them unclean, similar to lepers.

Most men of Jesus' day looked down on women, whether they were Jewish or gentile. Other than one's wife or mother, women were considered to be unworthy of a man's attention. Knowing this, you can understand a Samaritan woman's shock when a Jewish man asked her to draw him a drink of water from a well.

The Samaritan woman said to him, "You are a Jew and
I am a Samaritan woman. How can you ask me for a
drink?"…

Jesus answered her, "If you knew the gift of God and who it is that asks you for a drink, you would have asked him and he would have given you living water."

"Sir," the woman said, "you have nothing to draw with and the well is deep. Where can you get this living water?" (John 4:9–11)

One can imagine the woman's next question conveyed cynicism: "Are you greater than our father Jacob, who gave us the well and drank from it himself, as did also his sons and his flocks and herds?" (verse 12). Jesus conveyed spiritual truth in His answer: "Everyone who drinks this water will be thirsty again, but whoever drinks the water I give him will never thirst. Indeed, the water I give him will become in him a spring of water welling up to eternal life" (verses 13–14).

At first, the woman couldn't care less about eternal life, but she liked the sound of a type of water that would forever quench her thirst. That type of water would free her from the hard work of walking to the well to fetch water and carry it back home. She said, "Sir, give me this water so that I won't get thirsty and have to keep coming here to draw water" (verse 15). She apparently believed there was something about this stranger that could enable Him to give her miracle water. Then to her surprise, He changed the direction of the conversation. Jesus told her, "Go, call your husband and come back" (verse 16). She didn't hesitate to admit, "I have no husband" (verse 17). Jesus answered, "You are right when you say you have no husband. The fact is, you have had five husbands, and the man you now have is not your husband. What you have just said is quite true" (verses 17–18).

That is when the light came on for the woman. This was no

mere man she was talking to. She said, "Sir, I can see that you are a prophet" (verse 19). Suddenly she lost her interest in water, even though she hadn't taken a drink. Realizing she was in the presence of a prophet, she decided to ask Him to clarify a religious question that had always troubled her. (It is also possible that she wanted to divert His attention away from the embarrassing truth about her promiscuity.) She said to Jesus, "Our fathers worshiped on this mountain, but you Jews claim that the place where we must worship is in Jerusalem" (verse 20).

Jesus answered, "Believe me, woman, a time is coming when you will worship the Father neither on this mountain nor in Jerusalem. You Samaritans worship what you do not know; we worship what we do know, for salvation is from the Jews. Yet a time is coming and has now come when the true worshipers will worship the Father in spirit and truth, for they are the kind of worshipers the Father seeks. God is spirit, and his worshipers must worship in spirit and in truth" (verses 21–24).

When she heard these words, the woman's heart and mind were changed even further. Thinking about how firmly Jesus had proclaimed these truths about God and how He had known about her life and her adultery, she thought He might be more than a mere prophet. She identified Him as someone no one else had yet recognized—even His disciples. She didn't want to say this outright, so she approached the subject indirectly. "'I know that Messiah' (called Christ) 'is coming. When he comes, he will explain everything to us.'" Without a moment's hesitation, Jesus declared, "I who speak to you am he" (verses 25–26).

Wow! He was speaking to a woman who was a Samaritan and an adulteress. From a human standpoint, especially to first-century Jews, she was the most unlikely person to see that Jesus was God's Son, the anointed One. But this is who Jesus chose to reveal His identity to—a godless, self-centered, deceitful adulteress. And look at her response. She didn't raise objections or ask for proof. She was so overcome that she completely forgot why she had walked to the well. She forgot her water jar and went back to town to tell everyone she knew what had just happened. Her focus was no longer on herself—she wanted to spread the amazing news to everyone. She said, "Come, see a man who told me everything I ever did. Could this be the Christ?" (verse 29).

We are told, "They came out of the town and made their way toward him.... Many of the Samaritans from that town believed in him because of the woman's testimony, 'He told me everything I ever did'" (verses 30, 39). When men came out from the town to listen to Jesus, they begged Him to remain with them. He stayed with them two more days, and we are told that because of His teachings, many more became believers (see verses 40–41).

The woman's life was amazingly transformed. She had been born again. A woman who cared only about herself became a follower of Christ. And equally exciting, she lost all fear of others and their possible ridicule. She told the townsmen that she had likely found the Messiah. Some might wonder, *How do we know she was born again, considering her statement to the men was "Could this be the Christ?"* The answer is that she said it in the form of a question to avoid an argument. She knew that men, feeling superior to a woman, would never allow her to instruct them, especially about such a lofty thing as the appearance of the Messiah. So she wisely made her declaration in the form of a question. And yet her testimony was so convincing that the Spirit of God opened the men's hearts and empowered them to believe.

JESUS' PROMISES TO ALL WHO EMBRACE AND OBEY HIS WORDS

1. You will become His true disciple (see John 8:31).
2. You will receive knowledge of the truth (see John 8:32).
3. You will be liberated from enslavement to sin (see John 8:32–36).
4. You will gain intimacy with Jesus, the Son, and God the Father (see John 14:21).
5. You will be loved by the Father and Son in a special way (see John 14:21).
6. Jesus will reveal Himself to you (see John 14:21).
7. The Father and Son will come to you (see John 14:23).
8. The Father and Son will make Their home with you (see John 14:23).
9. You will be cleansed from your sin (see John 15:3).

10. Your prayers will be answered (see John 15:7).

11. You will bear much eternal fruit (see John 15:8).

12. You will dwell or remain in His love (see John 15:10).

13. Jesus' joy will be in you (see John 15:11).

14. Your joy will be full—complete, overflowing (see John 15:11).

15. Your "house" or life will not be destroyed (see Matthew 7:25).

16. Your life will be built on the perfect foundation (see Matthew 7:24; Luke 6:48).

17. You will be intimately known by Him (see Matthew 7:24–25).

18. You will have assurance of your eternal life (see Luke 6:46–48).

19. Your life and faith will not be shaken (see Luke 6:48).

20. You'll have ongoing infusion of spirit and life (see John 6:63).

NOTES

The epigraph for the book is taken from John 17:3, NKJV.

1. Steven K. Scott, *The Greatest Words Ever Spoken: Everything Jesus Said About You, Your Life, and Everything Else* (Colorado Springs: WaterBrook, 2008).

2. Frank Newport, "Americans More Likely to Believe in God Than the Devil, Heaven More Than Hell," Gallup News Service, June 13, 2007, www.gallup.com/poll/27877/americans-more-likely-believe-god-than-devil-heaven-more-than-hell.aspx.

3. Newport, "Americans More Likely to Believe in God."

4. A note to pastors: Do you feel caught between a rock and a hard place? Does your heart's desire to focus on the realities of following Christ keep getting crowded out by church programs and the expectations and demands of your board and members or the church's mortgage and budgetary needs? You don't need to bring radical changes overnight. Instead, focus on a gradual transition so that your priorities shift more and more toward teaching your people how to follow Christ.

5. A note to those in the pews: Just because your church is steeped in activities and programs doesn't mean you have to go in search of a different church. Work with your pastor and others to begin to transition the congregation's focus and priorities away from programs so you can start to discover and obey what Jesus taught.

6. Elisabeth Elliot, *Shadow of the Almighty: The Life and Testament of Jim Elliot* (New York: Harper and Row, 1958).

7. Russell Kelso Carter, "Standing on the Promises," 1886, http://library.timelesstruths.org/music/Standing_on_the _Promises/.

8. See Scott, *The Greatest Words Ever Spoken,* 298–304.

9. Keep in mind that a casual understanding of Jesus' commands, or mere intellectual agreement with His teachings, does not constitute belief as that word is used in Scripture. The ancient Greek word for belief, *pisteuo,* means to "totally trust, rely upon, and commit to."

10. Josephus lived circa 37–100 AD.

11. Peter W. Stoner and Robert C. Newman, *Science Speaks: Scientific Proof of the Accuracy of Prophecy and the Bible,* rev. ed. (Chicago: Moody Press, 2005), www.sciencespeaks.net.

12. C. S. Lewis, *Mere Christianity* (San Francisco: HarperSan-Francisco, 2001), 52.

13. Lewis, *Mere Christianity,* 52.

14. Josh McDowell, *Evidence That Demands a Verdict: Historical Evidences for the Christian Faith* (San Bernardino, CA: Here's Life, 1977), 127.

15. Gloria Gaither, "Let Freedom Ring" (Alexandria, IN: Gaither Copyright Management, 1982), www.musicnotes .com/sheetmusic/mtdVPE.asp?ppn=MN0066336.

OTHER BOOKS BY STEVEN K. SCOTT

The Greatest Words Ever Spoken

The Greatest Man Who Ever Lived

The Richest Man Who Ever Lived

Mentored by a Millionaire

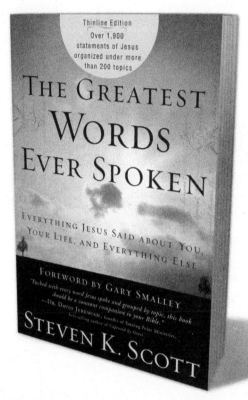

Believers have been inspired by His deity.
Now they can be mentored by His humanity!

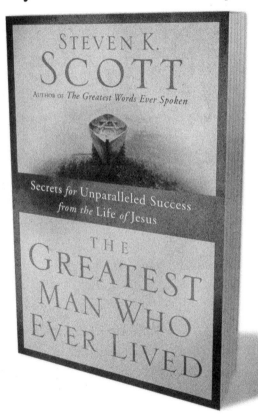

Best-selling author Steven K. Scott inspires readers with life lessons from Jesus' years on earth, revealing the most authoritative, inspiring, and practical model for personal success.

Read an excerpt from this book and more at WaterBrookMultnomah.com!

Put the Wisdom of Solomon to Work in Your Life

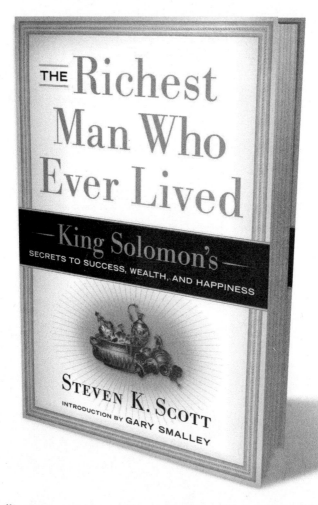

Multimillionaire entrepreneur Steven K. Scott explores and applies the biblical wisdom of Proverbs to mentor you into a life of extraordinary personal, relational, spiritual, and financial success.

Read an excerpt from this book and more at WaterBrookMultnomah.com!